D0457617

Good stories but
does go off the deep
end by the end of the
Book.

Great Communities. Healthy Environments. By Design.

STRANGE POWERS OF PETS

by Brad Steiger
& Sherry Hansen Steiger

DONALD I. FINE, INC.
New York

Copyright © 1992 by Brad Steiger and Sherry Hansen Steiger

All rights reserved, including the right of reproduction in whole or in part in any form. Published in the United States of America by Donald I. Fine, Inc. and in Canada by General Publishing Company Limited.

ISBN 1-55611-294-7

Manufactured in the United States of America

Designed by Irving Perkins Associates

Dedicated to the memory of Erling F. Olson, Brad Steiger's beloved father, who first taught him to respect the rights and the intelligence of all animals, and to the memory of Sherry's beloved son Erik Hansen, whose love of nature and concern for wildlife lives on in the hearts of all who knew him.

Contents

Part Two
THE LIFESAVERS, THE DEFENDERS, AND THE CRIMEBUSTERS

Part Three
EERIE ANIMAL TRACKS INTO THE TWILIGHT ZONE 109

Part One

THE MYSTERIOUS PSYCHIC BOND THAT LINKS PEOPLE AND THEIR PETS

Sunday and Savage—A Unique Love Bond Between Man and Monkey

Filmmaker Richard Savage, 66, lives in a remote preserve in British Columbia where bears and coyotes maintain their natural sovereignty over their wild kingdom. Not long ago, he reminisced about his years with a Capuchin monkey and the extraordinary love bond that had been forged between them.

"I was about to take out the garbage when my ten-year-old white-breasted Capuchin monkey, Sunday, began screeching and clutching at my hand," Savage said. "She made whimpering sounds that made the hair on the back of my neck stand up."

Savage told journalist Paul Bannister that he walked outside, but could see nothing. "Then, suddenly, a 700–pound grizzly bear lurched out of the trees and came lumbering toward me. He wanted my garbage. I dropped it and retreated quickly."

The filmmaker knew that Sunday's alarm had saved his life. "If she hadn't warned me," Savage acknowledged, "I could have been mauled to death. Yet Sunday could not have seen the big grizzly, and she had a poor sense of smell. I doubt if she could have heard him. I don't know how she was able to know that a violent death awaited me."

The next time Sunday sounded her distress signal, Savage paid immediate attention. On this occasion, the devoted animal kept running to the side of Savage's parked truck, making those same desperate whimpering sounds.

Savage got his rifle, once again expecting the charge of a large predator—but what he eventually discovered could have been even more life-threatening.

"I finally got down on my hands and knees beside the area of the truck where Sunday kept making these pathetic whimpering sounds. I was startled to find that I had ripped open a brake line on a rock and nearly all of the fluid had leaked out. If I had tried to drive down off the mountain, I would almost certainly have crashed and possibly have been killed."

Several months later, Savage and Sunday were speeding home in the truck when the Capuchin began vocalizing. "Once again," the filmmaker recalled, "it was that insistent whimpering that had warned me before of danger."

Savage stopped the truck, and watched curiously and cautiously as Sunday ran ahead about one hundred yards. He ran after her and found her off the side of the road in thick brush.

"I was astonished to find Sunday with her hands on the tiny, damp bundle of a newborn fawn," Savage said. "The doe was there, dead, hit by a car. We rescued the baby deer and took her the next day to a game refuge where she would be raised with others of her kind."

Savage has long puzzled over the manner in which Sunday could possibly have known the precise spot where the newborn deer lay. "Several miles before we even got to the spot, Sunday knew that the fawn needed our help."

Savage said that he would leave Sunday with Canadian author Philip Ormand whenever he was away on filmmaking assignments.

"It was uncanny," Ormand remembered. "Several minutes before Richard would telephone to talk to me, Sunday would jump up and start chattering. After his call, she would settle down for days, ignoring the telephone—until just before Richard called again. They had a very strong bond between them."

Sunday died several years ago, leaving Richard Savage sorrowing. But three nights after her death, he had awakened to feel the Capuchin's small, warm body snuggled against his shoulder in the way Sunday had cuddled in life.

"I knew then that she wasn't really gone," Savage said. "Our separation is just a temporary parting."

Her Psychic Cats Saved Her Life

When Sucile L.'s son Joe was around twelve years old, he brought home a beautiful little white kitty all covered with grease and told her that the kitten was her birthday gift.

Sucile's response was intended to be very firm: "Honey, we just can't have a cat."

"But, Mom," Joe frowned, "it's your birthday gift."

"So we cleaned the little kitty up," Sucile said. "I wrapped it in a towel and put it on my lap. She just curled up and seemed at home. By that time, I just couldn't give her up, so we kept the cat. Joe is twenty-three now, so you can figure out how long we had the cat."

Sucile and her children were living in South Dakota when the cat she christened Lucky came into her life. "As the years went by," she said, "I noticed that Lucky seemed to be very psychic. If it was a couple of hours before a storm or tornado was coming, she would run up my wall. I finally realized that she was warning me in advance of every storm.

"Lucky always used to lie on my tummy," Sucile continued. "I had some surgery, and when I came home, Lucky seemed to know and would not lie on my stomach, but only on my neck.

"I would say to her, 'If you love me, blink your eyes.' She would blink them twice, then look up at me and purr, touching me lightly with her paw."

After a few years, Sucile got another kitten as a playmate for Lucky, and she felt that both of the cats considered themselves her loyal guardians.

"The day that they gave their lives for me started out as a very quiet and peaceful summer's day," Sucile said. "I was sitting in my home in South Dakota, writing a letter, and Lucky and her friend were sitting on the window ledge, watching me.

"Suddenly a big storm came up, and I heard a loud crack as lightning struck a nearby tree.

"I looked up to see a big red ball outside my kitchen window. Somehow the lightning bolt had created the dangerous phenomenon of ball lightning. That deadly charge of electricity appeared about to pass through the window and to come directly for me."

Sucile will always remember how her beloved cats positioned themselves so that their bodies intercepted the ball lightning. "The cats just lit up. Their entire bodies glowed, and there was a bluish white aura around them as the lightning touched them. When the firemen came, they said they could not believe that the charge had not continued through the cats and hit me."

Sucile knows in her very core of being that her cats saved her life by intercepting the lightning's deadly charge. Miraculously, Lucky and her friend had survived the terrible shock, but they had lost their hair and were badly burned.

"My veterinarian told me that he knew that I loved my kitties, but if I really loved them, I would put them to sleep," Sucile concluded her story. "I allowed him to do so to prevent my darling cats from enduring any more suffering on my behalf."

Toby Knew His Master Was in Danger—Over Four Miles Away

Auto mechanic Josef Schwarzl, 47, of San Jose, California, does not hesitate to affirm that he owes his life to his golden Labrador, Toby.

One Sunday evening after a weekend of skiing, Schwarzl was working on his own car in his shop. "I was sitting in the car with the engine idling—which would have been fine if the building's extractor fan hadn't broken. To make matters even worse, because it was cold I had closed the garage doors."

Tired from the weekend's strenuous workout on the ski slopes, Schwarzl dozed off. The shop began filling with deadly carbon monoxide, and the auto mechanic could have died from the poison gas before anyone found him.

Toby, his golden Labrador, was at home with Schwarzl's mother, who was visiting him from her native Austria. "Toby became very agitated and began barking," Schwarzl said. "There was no way that Mom could quiet him. He kept running to the door, scratching wildly at it. When she let him out, he would run and turn and wait for her to follow."

Mrs. Schwarzl does not speak very much English, and she does not know how to operate a car, so she was unable to drive the four miles to Josef's garage to ask him what Toby wanted. Finally, desperate to quiet the dog, she went to a neighbor and asked him to drive them to the shop.

"They found me unconscious, with the car engine still pumping out deadly carbon monoxide," Schwarzl said. "Somehow Toby knew of the danger that I was in—and he saved my life!"

Rescued by a Rat

Former University of Toronto lecturer Ian Currie shared a remarkable instance of psychic bonding that had occurred between an elderly West Virginia coal miner and a rat that inhabited the dark tunnel.

"The old man, who owned a small mine and worked it himself, noticed that one particular rat would stay near him, as if keeping him company, while he worked at the coal face," Currie said. "Over a period of several months, the two became accustomed to one another.

"The miner would feed the rat from his lunch box, and when it came time to fire the shots that would bring down the coal face, he would chase the rat away so it would not be injured.

"One day, while the miner was working alone," Currie continued the account, "the rat appeared to be unduly agitated and kept scampering up to the miner, then running off. Intrigued, the man put down his drill and followed the rat around the corner to see if he could figure out what was bothering the creature. He had just moved away from the face when the roof collapsed—in the exact spot where he had been working."

The miner, according to Currie, would certainly have been killed without the rat's warning. "But how the rat knew the roof was about to collapse and why he warned the man is presently one of the mysteries of animal-human interaction. I think," Currie added, "that the rat employed an animal's intuition for danger, and somehow it was able to communicate with the human who had befriended him."

His Kindness to a Horse Really Paid Off

Los Angeles architect and photographer Kelvin Jones, 39, was vacationing at the Guadalupe Ranch in Douglas, Arizona, and was helping round up several yearlings that had strayed into a steep canyon. Lacking only experience, not enthusiasm, Jones was uncertain how to handle his horse when it started slipping on loose shale. The horse bolted and Jones was thrown.

"I hurt my ankle very badly, and I couldn't even stand, much less walk on it," Jones said. "I was in a very bad situation, because the area was full of rattlesnakes and mountain lions. What was even worse, I wasn't likely to be missed for a day or more."

But help would come to Jones from an unexpected source. Back at the ranch, a quarter horse named Smoke began acting restless in the corral.

"What's the matter with old Smoke?" one of the cowhands asked his buddy.

"Danged if I know," the other replied. "He's generally the quietest horse of the bunch."

In the next few moments, much to the amazement of the ranchhands, Smoke had broken down a section of the corral and had taken off across the high chaparal in a dead run.

"Good gravy," one of the men shouted to the other. "Let's saddle up fast and bring old Smoke back to the corral before these other critters think they can take off like he did."

"It was a strange kind of miracle," Jones recalled. "Smoke was the first horse that I had learned to ride when I arrived at the Guadalupe Ranch. I would always make a fuss over him, and we became good friends. Soon after I fell, it seems that he broke out of his corral and set off to cover the seven or eight miles to where I was."

There was no way that the two ranchhands could catch Smoke. The horse seemed to know exactly where it was going, and they could only follow in angry pursuit.

"When Smoke found me, there were two hot and boiling-mad cowboys chasing him," Jones said. "Their anger soon changed to astonishment when they saw that Smoke had led them directly to a ranch guest who was in terrible trouble. It became clear to all of us that he had broken out of his corral to come to rescue me."

That night, after a doctor had seen to his ankle, Kelvin Jones presented Smoke with a special reward: a large bag of apples.

The German Shepherd Who Cried for Help from the Dog Pound

Campbell, California, real estate agent Irmgard Auckerman will never forget the day when she received an urgent, insistent telepathic cry for help from her German shepherd Wolfgang.

Ms. Auckerman had just returned from an out-of-town business trip, and she stopped by her home to check up on a few things. She had left Wolfie with her ex-husband, so she dialed his number to see if it would be convenient for her to stop by his place and pick up her dog later.

"My ex had left his answering machine on, so I just left a message that I was home and, since he wasn't, I would leave Wolfie with him for another day," Ms. Auckerman said.

"It was while I was driving to my office that I felt a strong message inside my head that I could not at first comprehend. Although the thoughts and impressions were jumbled, the meaning was quite clear: Something was very urgent; something was very deadly and dangerous."

Ms. Auckerman stopped at a gas station and called her daughter. "I was relieved to hear that she was fine, but I kept receiving a message of approaching danger."

She decided to phone ahead to her office to see if anyone had left any messages there for her. Nothing.

Ms. Auckerman returned to her automobile, and when she put the car into gear it was as if another intelligence took control of the steering wheel.

"I drove all the way across town without having any idea where I was going," she said. "It was only when I pulled up in front of the Humane Society that I realized immediately where I was and what I was doing."

She knew then that her beloved German shepherd Wolfie was somehow in the pound and about to be put to death. She overrode the conscious knowledge that Wolfie was safe at her ex-husband's place. She had no doubt that Wolfgang had sent her a desperate cry for help and had somehow called her to come to his rescue.

It took Ms. Auckerman twenty minutes to find Wolfgang. "The people in charge there told me that if I had arrived another hour later, it would have been too late. Wolfie had been there unclaimed without his dog tags for seventy-two hours, and that is their cut-off time. He was already slated to be put to sleep within the hour. Wolfie sent me a cry for help. He must have known that he was going to die, and he telepathically communicated with me."

Later, Ms. Auckerman got the full story from her ex-husband: "He had come home one day to discover that Wolfie was gone. He thought that I had come back from my business trip earlier than expected and that I had picked him up. Actually, Wolfie had slipped out of the house and had gone for an unauthorized walk.

"Somehow, Wolfie had lost his dog tags, and he got picked up by the dog catchers and taken to the pound. The Humane Society keeps unclaimed, untagged dogs for only seventy-two hours, so Wolfie's time was already running out very fast when I first arrived home."

Ms. Auckerman still shudders to think of what would have happened to her wonderful canine friend if she had not received Wolfie's telepathic cry for help. "If I had continued to believe him safe at my ex-husband's, I would have decided to leave him there for another day—and that decision would have been fatal for Wolfie."

Even if she had discovered Wolfgang was missing immediately upon her return home, Ms. Auckerman realizes that she would not have had any idea where to search for him if it had not been for the telepathic directions that somehow made her drive directly to the Humane Society. Truly, this case stands as an astonishing example of human-animal psychic communication.

Larry Dossey, a medical doctor who has authored the fascinating *Recovering the Soul—A Scientific and Spiritual Search*, remarks that it would be difficult to convince millions of pet owners that they do not on occasion "communicate" with their dogs, cats, birds, or even their goldfish. "Everyone," he comments, "has felt at one time or another on the same 'wavelength' with an animal."

Dr. Dossey suggests that millions of pet lovers may be convinced that their pets may be "part human" because of a universal mind that connects human beings, animals, and all other living things. Many pet owners have come to believe completely in a totality that envelops all beings. Telepathy would be an easy task to accomplish if the minds of all living creatures were somehow united in a great universal mind pool.

Dr. Dossey quotes J. Allen Boone, the movie producer and the former head of RKO studios, and the author of *Kinship with All Life*. It was Boone who shared so eloquently his experiences with

Strongheart, the international champion German shepherd and movie celebrity.

When Boone first gained possession of the shepherd, he was advised to interact with him as if he were an intelligent human being. He was admonished to say nothing to him that he did not feel in his heart. And, interestingly, he was told to read something worthwhile to Strongheart each day.

Boone was astonished when the two of them dealt with a conflict of lifestyle by his first explaining his problem to Strongheart, who then pantomimed his response.

"For the first time," Boone said, "I was actually conscious of being in rational correspondence with an animal. . . . I had been privileged to watch an animal acting upon its own initiative, put into expression qualities of independent thinking, clear reasoning, good judgment, foresight, prudence, and common sense. I had been taught to believe these qualities belonged more or less exclusively to the members of the 'educated members' of our species."

The scientist in Dr. Dossey cautions him to point out that a great number of alleged instances of human-animal communication can be explained by ordinary sensory clues that the pet has learned to identify. But we are quite certain that Dr. Dossey has in mind such cases as those we share in this book when he comments:

"It makes good biological sense that a nonlocal, psychological communion might have evolved between humans and animals as an asset to survival, then the stories of returning animals, precognitive gerbils, and talented flies may be more than amusing parlor tales. They may be indicators that nature in its wisdom would, in fact, have designed a mind that envelops all creatures great and small."

Strange Powers That Help Lost Pets Come Home

In February 1966, Blackie, a fifteen-pound black Persian cat that had been accidentally left in Florida by Mr. and Mrs. Richard Bower during Thanksgiving of the year before, found its way back to their home in Forked River, New Jersey.

In the spring of 1966, a dog named Smokey found its owners, Mr. and Mrs. Phillip R. Bean of Seattle, after having been parted from them for three and a half years—and after the Beans had twice changed their place of residence.

When the Hutchinson family moved from Niagara Falls, New York, to Indianapolis in October of 1988, they left their beagle Oscar with a grandson who was extremely fond of the dog. Although four-year-old Oscar had never left the confines of the neighborhood in Niagara Falls, he arrived at the Hutchinson's new home in Indiana seven months later. Lean and bedraggled, his footpads raw and bloody, Oscar proved that he loved his owners more than he esteemed the place at which they had left him.

Baby Overcame Epileptic Seizures and Her Masters' Change of Home to Return to the Donegan Family

Baby, a cocker spaniel-poodle mix that suffered from epileptic seizures, managed to find its way back to the John Donegan family of Addison, Illinois, on September 9, 1969, after having been dog-napped and held for eight months. To complicate matters for Baby, the Donegans had moved to Addison from Melrose Park in the interim, and the dog had first to find the trailer home of Mrs. Catherine Geitz, Mrs. Donegan's mother, to appeal for help.

In recounting the story for the Chicago *Tribune*, Donegan theorized that the dognappers were puzzled when Baby had one of her epileptic fits. "They didn't understand what it was, and they threw her out."

Mrs. Geitz, Mrs. Donegan's mother, lived over fifteen miles from the Donegans' new home; but Baby had visited "Grandma's" house with the family before she had been dognapped.

Mrs. Donegan said that Baby looked terrible when she arrived at her mother's trailer. "Her nose was sunburned and swollen, her feet were raw, and two back teeth were broken. But it was our Baby! She still had her dog tags on. Now our family is back together."

The Amazing Saga of Hector, The Stowaway Dog

Walt Disney Productions created an unforgettable film classic in *Incredible Journey*, the true yarn about two dogs and a cat that somehow managed to find their way through a strange wilderness to arrive at their human family's new home several hundred miles from the old homestead. It is indeed a loss to the lovers of animal lore that no studio has yet filmed the true account of the incredible journey of Hector, the large black-and-white terrier, that accomplished one of the greatest feats in the annals of pets-that-came-home tales.

Second Officer Harold Kildall of the SS *Hanley* was busy seeing to the loading of cargo on the morning of April 20, 1922, when he saw the black-and-white terrier walking up the gangplank. The dog paced about on deck, sniffed at a number of various objects, then returned to shore on the Government Dock in Vancouver, Washington.

From time to time that day, Kildall noticed the large terrier inspecting the four other ships at dock. He was intrigued by the curious actions of the dog and by the air of a genuine sense of purpose that it exhibited, but he was too busy to pay the animal more than casual attention, for the *Hanley* was getting ready to ship out.

The next day, when the ship was on its way to Yokohama, Second Officer Kildall was surprised to discover that the big black-and-white terrier had somehow managed to stow away aboard ship.

Fortunately for Hector, Captain Warner liked dogs and didn't sentence the terrier to be thrown overboard as food for the sharks. Both he and his crew made the terrier welcome.

Although Hector was willing to work for his fare—he stood watch with Second Officer Kildall each night—he remained aloof, refusing to express any kind of affection toward any of the crew members.

Three weeks later, the SS *Hanley* was unloading timber in Yokohama Bay. Kildall could not help noticing the terrier's behavior as their vessel pulled up next to the SS *Simaloer*, a Dutch ship that was also unloading timber.

Two officers and some crewmen from the Dutch ship boarded a sampan and began to move toward the customs landing. As the sampan passed close to the *Hanley*, Hector began to leap about and bark excitedly. At the same time, one of the passengers of the sampan spotted the big terrier and began to wave his arms and shout.

Within moments, Hector was reunited with his master, Willem H.

Mante, second officer of the *Simaloer*. The man and his devoted dog had been separated at the Government Dock in Vancouver, and the Dutch ship had sailed away before Mante could find Hector.

One can only guess at the remarkable ability that enabled the big black-and-white terrier to select the one ship among many at the dock in Vancouver that would take him across the ocean to the precise spot where his master would be waiting. It is as if Hector's very heart was attuned to that of Second Officer Mante.

Years later, Captain Kenneth Dobson, USN, became so intrigued by the story of Hector that he set about checking the accounts of all the witnesses on both vessels. Hector's master, Willem H. Mante, told him that as an inveterate dog lover, he had had several dogs after the death of Hector, but none of them could ever take his place. "I'll never forget the faith and friendship of that one-man, one-ship dog, Hector," Mante said.

In Dodson's book, *Hector, the Stowaway Dog*, the naval officer speculates as to what mysterious instinct could have governed the dog's methodical search for the one ship out of so many that would carry him across an ocean to rejoin Mante, his beloved master. "Did the character of the *Hanley*'s cargo and perhaps other signs tell him that the *Hanley* was bound for the same destination as his own ship?" Captain Dodson wonders. "Did he then attach himself to the officer whose duties were like his master's? Any answers would be only the guesswork of men who know only *what* happened."

The Remarkable Journey of Li-Ping

It is always sad, and sometimes traumatic, when circumstances arise that force one to part from a beloved pet. In April of 1955, when Vivian Allgood, a registered nurse, had to move from Sandusky, Ohio, to Orlando, Florida, because of a job change, she was forced to leave Li-Ping, her beautiful black cat, behind in the care of her sister.

While Ms. Allgood went about the business of making the appropriate adjustments to her new job in Orlando, Li-Ping was not taking the separation nearly as well. He moped around his new turf for a couple of weeks—and then, to the horror of Ms. Allgood's sister, he vanished.

One evening in May, about a month after she had moved to Orlando, Vivian Allgood was sitting on a friend's porch when her attention was drawn to a sorry, bedraggled cat that was limping its painful way along the street. There was just *something* about the cat that made her think about her dear Li-Ping, left back in Sandusky.

Following one of those strange whims that seem to come from nowhere, Vivian called out the name Li-Ping. Both she and her friend were astonished to see the cat stop dead in its tracks, turn to the sound of her voice, then come limping and stumbling to her just as fast as its punished condition would allow.

Within moments, the cat was in Ms. Allgood's arms, and she was jubilantly shouting that it was indeed Li-Ping!

Her friend wanted to know: how could that be possible? How could a cat leave Sandusky, Ohio, with no knowledge of the present whereabouts of its mistress and find its way to the very street on which she lived in a strange state and city?

Many cats look a great deal alike, Ms. Allgood's friend noted. Perhaps this poor cat, scarred, scratched, and skinned, simply looked like Li-Ping.

Vivian appraised the shabby condition of the cat in her arms. Large hunks of hair had been torn from its body. It had obviously survived innumerable fights to the finish. Its feet were raw and bleeding from the terribly long walk—1,586 miles!

But Vivian Allgood knew that it was Li-Ping, who had no voice—only a strange kind of rasping sound. And as she lovingly repeated his name amidst welcoming tears of joy, this cat could make only a faint, little rasping cry.

Each day for a week, Vivian Allgood gave her incredible cat his fill of milk and liver until his many wounds and his sore feet began to heal.

How Li-Ping could have found his way to a destination beyond his possible experience or knowledge cannot be explained. Li-Ping had never been to Orlando with his mistress. He had no awareness about where Ms. Allgood had moved. And it is unlikely that he could have read a road map even if he did hear the name "Orlando, Florida."

The Exiled "Killer Cat" That Found Its Way Home to Forgiveness

In June of 1989, Murka suddenly became a "killer cat" and ate two pet canaries prized by her owner, Olga Stravinsky of Moscow.

Because of her love for Murka, Mrs. Stravinsky did not have the heart to practice an eye for an eye and to have the cat put to death. Instead she pronounced exile for the naughty tortoiseshell and banished her from their Moscow apartment to the home of relatives in far-off industrial Voronezh.

By November, however, Murka had returned to the Stravinsky apartment, foot-weary and decidedly the worse for wear. She had lost a hunk out of one ear and several inches off her tail.

Other family members pleaded Murka's case, but Mrs. Stravinsky's heart had already been touched, and she had granted forgiveness from the sentence of exile.

It was also apparent that Murka had found time for a little more than walking and fighting during the 450 miles back home. A family member appraised her rounded frame and her carefully measured gait and assessed the obvious fact that kittens would soon be making an appearance.

Sugar Would Not Be Left Behind

Early in 1950, the Stacy W. Woods family moved from Gage, Oklahoma, to Anderson, California, taking with them their yellow cat, Sugar. Then, in June 1951, the Woodses decided to return to Gage. Not wishing to uproot Sugar once again, they reluctantly left their pet with a friend with whom the cat had established a good relationship.

In August 1952, fourteen months later, Mr. and Mrs. Woods were milking in their barn in Gage, Oklahoma, when a cat suddenly jumped through an open window and landed on Mrs. Woods' shoulder. To her astonishment, the creature began to rub itself against her neck in a familiar manner, purring joyously.

Taking the cat into both hands for a closer examination, she excitedly announced to her husband that the begrimed, bedraggled, exhausted cat was their Sugar come home.

In an article in the April 1954 issue of *Frontiers: A Magazine of Natural History*, Woods said that he could not believe that a cat could find its way back home over a distance of nearly 1,400 miles. Then he remembered that their Sugar had a peculiarly deformed hipbone that had been the result of a broken right rear leg sustained in her kittenhood. He ran his hand over the cat's flank and found the familiar deformity. There was no longer any question that Sugar had come home.

Dognapped, Skippy Escaped to Walk 600 Miles Back Home

In his book *Strange World*, Frank Edwards, the late master compiler of astounding true events, writes of a dog named Skippy that vanished from its home in Mount Clemens, Michigan, the apparent victim of a dognapper.

Skippy returned to his astonished and delighted owner six months later with a dog tag that had been issued in Fort Dodge, Iowa. How had the dog managed to find his way six hundred miles back home when he had never even been out of Mount Clemens before his dognapping?

Tommy Wanted To Go Back—Even If It Meant Crossing the Mississippi River

When the Robert M. Drewry family moved to Fort Worth, Texas, from Haleyville, Alabama, they brought their three-year-old tabby, Tommy, with them. But Tommy was clearly unhappy in the Lone Star State. One day he failed to show up for his dinner in the new home; and several weeks later, Tommy was seen walking around the old, familiar haunts in Haleyville.

How can anyone explain how the tabby could have found his way back over six hundred miles—which included a crossing of the Mississippi River?

Sophia, the Duck That Preferred Its Human Family

Frank Edwards points out that dogs and cats are not the only pets that demonstrate a remarkable homing instinct. The J. W. Meehan family in Los Angeles had a pet duck named Sophia that they had raised since she left the egg. Feeling that she needed the company of those of her own kind, the Meehans drove Sophia to Echo Park Lake and released her to be among her fellow ducks.

It soon became apparent that in her own mind, Sophia was a member of the Meehan family. Somehow, she made it back home to their house on Seventh Avenue, nine miles through heavy Los Angeles traffic.

Lost En Route to Home, Stubby Walked 1,000 Miles To Return to His Mute and Crippled Mistress

On April 5, 1950, the International News Service carried the moving account of how Stubby had made a thousand-mile-trek from the Indiana-Illinois border to his home in Colorado Springs, Colorado.

Stubby's return was especially poignant because his thirteen-year-old mistress Della Shaw had been crippled and dumb since birth. Stubby, Della's constant companion, had been the sunshine of her life until he vanished on that terrible day in 1948.

Della and her grandmother, Mrs. Harry McKinzie, had been visiting relatives in Indianapolis on an extended four-month stay.

They had set out for home in a truck containing some furniture; and somewhere along the way, most likely between Indianapolis and Decatur, Illinois, Stubby had become separated from the vehicle.

Della's family had horrible visions of her beloved pet falling out of the truck and being mangled on the highway. The grief that a pet lover suffers when a cherished animal is lost may well be compounded in the heart of a handicapped child. Although Della was mute, her grandparents could feel so strongly her silent sorrow over the loss of her devoted Stubby.

Harry McKinzie took out newspaper ads in cities along the route that his wife and granddaughter had taken home to Colorado Springs. He contacted several friends to ask their assistance in attempting to locate the missing dog.

Months passed without any results. It appeared as though the faithful Stubby had been killed as the result of a fall from the truck. Della was slowly adjusting to life without Stubby and valiantly attempting to overcome the terrible loneliness that he had left in her heart.

In late March of 1950, eighteen months after Stubby's disappearance on the ill-fated trip from Indianapolis, Harry McKinzie happened to walk by the old house in Colorado. Incredibly, there was Stubby sitting on the sidewalk, staring vacantly into space, as if awaiting some command or signal.

McKinzie said that the dog was dirty and dazed, his body bloated from hunger. His footpads were swollen and bleeding, painful testimony to his long journey home.

Although Stubby seemed scarcely to recognize McKinzie, when Harry presented him to Della the dog rallied and began lavishing his mistress with soft whines and "kisses." Della's eyes expressed her great love and her gratitude that some miracle had brought Stubby back to her arms.

Harry McKinzie told the International News Service that they knew that Della was happy once again. "We can tell by the look on her face. And once Stubby gets all the food and sleep he needs, he'll be his old self again."

2,500 Miles To Find Its New Home—
A Long-Distance Record For Felines!

In their book *The Strange World of Animals and Pets*, Vincent and Margaret Gaddis recount the story of the cat that traversed at least twenty-five hundred miles to be reunited with its owners, thus establishing a long-distance record for an act of feline devotion.

In 1949, Mr. and Mrs. Charles B. Smith decided to move to San Gabriel, California, from their home in St. Petersburg, Florida. Perhaps because they had once read that cats often develop an allegiance to places rather than to people, the Smiths elected to spare their Tom the trauma of a long-distance move and the disruption of his normal routine. Robert Hanson, the purchaser of their St. Petersburg home, appeared to develop a rapport with Tom, so the Smiths made the decision to leave the cat with him.

Two weeks after they had relocated to San Gabriel, however, they received a letter from Hanson bearing the sad news that Tom had run away. It seems quite likely at that point that the Smiths deeply regretted their decision to abandon their faithful friend.

One afternoon in early August, 1951, two years and six weeks after the move to California, Mrs. Smith was annoyed by the sound of a cat wailing in the yard.

Assigned to chase the noisy intruder out of their yard, Mr. Smith was amazed when, instead of running away, the cat ran toward him and leaped into his arms. It took him only a moment to recognize their Tom.

Mrs. Smith was skeptical. They had left a well-fed, sleek cat with Robert Hanson. This scraggly creature was skinny, worn, and frazzled—and so weak that it collapsed on the kitchen floor. Its fur was bleached by the sun and came out by the handfuls. Its paws were bloody and covered with scabs.

"Then we thought of a sure test," the Gaddises write. "Tom had been raised on baby food and had developed an unusual fondness for Pablum. [Mrs. Smith] put a saucer of it on the floor and, exhausted though he was, the battered cat dived into it up to his whiskers."

Mrs. Smith was now convinced that their old Tom had found his way from St. Petersburg, Florida, to San Gabriel, California, a distance of 2,500 miles, to once again become a member of their family circle. "We were certainly glad to see him," she said. "And Tom was happy too when he dropped into a well-deserved sleep beside his empty dish."

Joker Set Sail for the South Pacific

On January 20, 1958, the Associated Press carried an account of the journey of a cocker spaniel named Joker that rivals that of Hector the Stowaway Dog.

During World War II, Army Captain Stanley C. Raye received his orders for overseas duty in the South Pacific. He had no choice other than to leave his cocker spaniel in his Pittsburg, California home. Joker was despondent. He spent a lackluster two weeks moping, then he disappeared.

Two army doctors reported seeing the stray dog in Oakland, about thirty miles from Joker's home in Pittsburg. Somehow, he managed to stow away aboard an army transport. Joker was about to be destroyed when a sympathetic army major volunteered to adopt him.

The transport made several ports of call, and at each docking Joker was at the helm to sniff the air and to examine the seaport. It was not until the ship reached one particular South Pacific island that Joker jumped ship and raced ashore. Although the cocker spaniel was pursued, he could not be deterred until he was barking joyfully at the feet of an overwhelmed Captain Raye.

Joker's adoptive master could not dispute the dog's obvious elation at his reunion with the captain. It was apparent to all observers that the courageous cocker spaniel had found his true master. Without rancor, the major relinquished his claim on Joker.

How Joker managed to find Captain Raye presents an almost unfathomable mystery. All the dog knew was that his beloved master had left him. How could he have known that the captain had been assigned to a faraway island in the Pacific Ocean?

Since Joker had never been on board a ship of any kind, what unseen force led him to the Oakland port so that he might stow away aboard a vessel that would take him to Captain Raye? What greater intelligence told Joker which island was harboring his master among the many at which the transport stopped?

Captain Raye and Joker were inseparable until the remarkable animal died early in 1958 at Great Falls, Montana. Joker had lived a full and rich fourteen and one-half years, and many were the researchers who wished that it had been possible sometime during that long life span to have solved the mystery of how Joker had accomplished his seemingly impossible mission of reunion.

How Do They Find Their Way Home?

One of the most famous of all the accounts of animals that found their way back to home, hearth, and heart after conquering what would seem to have been insurmountable odds is that of Bobbie the collie, who made his way alone and on foot from Indiana to Oregon. When Colonel E. Hofer, president of the Oregon Humane Society, launched an investigation of Bobbie's fantastic journey, he received hundreds of letters from men and women who had assisted or befriended the dog on its amazing trek westward. It was from such accounts that Charles Alexander was able to document the story in his book, *Bobbie: A Great Collie of Oregon*. Incredibly, when the complete tale had been pieced together and Bobbie's trail was plotted on maps, it was found that the collie had managed to pick a very reasonable route with few detours.

Dr. Larry Dossey states that the reason that we assess as a great mystery such accounts of pets making their way to their masters across land previously unknown to them lies in our assumption that the ". . . animal mind is confined to its brain, and that it therefore cannot know 'at a distance.' Alternately, if the animal mind were not confined to points in space (its own brain and body) or time (the present moment), it would be free to scan space and time and gain knowledge of 'the way home' over trails it never traveled before."

Dr. Dossey, a physician of internal medicine with the Dallas Diagnostic Association and a former chief of staff of Medical City Dallas Hospital, finds another possible explanation of how animals return over great distances in shamanism and telepathy. In his thought-provoking book, *Recovering the Soul—A Scientific and Spiritual Search*, Dr. Dossey reflects:

"If the record from shamanism is correct and meaningful inter-species communication does exist between humans and animals, then human knowledge of 'the way back' could conceivably be shared with the animal mind. Thus in the . . . case of Bobbie, the lost female collie, the information how to travel from her home in Ohio to the new residence in Oregon, where she had never been, could have been conveyed to her by her owners, who did know the way."

Dr. Dossey's suggestion of a "nonlocal mind" implies that we and our pets, with our individual minds, are parts of "something larger that we cannot claim as our own private possession."

To fully understand and embrace this concept requires a genuine humility—humility that allows us ". . . to know deeply that consciousness is not the sole possession of an ego; that it is shared by not only other persons, but perhaps by other living things as well. It is humility that allows us to take seriously the possibility that we may be on a similar footing with all the rest of God's creatures."

Kinship with all creatures of the earth, sky, and water is an integral element in the practice of American Indian Medicine Power, and such a respect for all life forms is also manifest in the teachings of such Christian mystics as St. Francis of Assisi.

If we find the idea of the nonlocal, unbounded One Mind foreign to us, Dr. Dossey warns, ". . . the reason may be that we have gradually lost our connection with the natural world. As a consequence, our world is now gravely imperiled by our . . . lack of sensitivity to the whole. . . . If we wish to preserve our world, we must first find our Mind by recovering our connections with the heavens and the Earth . . . to begin once more to talk, with St. Francis, to the creatures."

Dramatic Proofs of a Human-Feline Psychic Bond

Dr. Franklin R. Ruehl, a nuclear physicist and author who is well known for his articles on science for the layman, has often pondered whether or not humans can actually establish a psychic link with animals. "Is the concept of interspecies telepathic communication totally illogical?" he has asked as a lead-in to his popular Los Angeles-based cable television program, "Mysteries from Beyond the Other Dominion." "An an affirmative answer appears applicable to the former interrogative," he concludes, "based on the results of an extensive battery of experiments conducted by Duke University researchers back in 1978."

Dr. Ruehl went on to explain that Stuart Harary was an undergraduate student majoring in psychology at Duke who claimed to be able to project himself into an out-of-body-experience (OBE) at will. In order to test him, he was placed in either of two rooms in Durham, North Carolina—one at Duke and the other in Building A at the Psychical Research Foundation (PRF). A kitten, who had previously exhibited a rapport with Harary, was placed in a target room in Building B, which Harary's out-of-body spirit was to visit. Building A was some fifty feet from Building B and a quarter of a mile from Duke University.

Researchers had noted that normally the kitten, who was just seven weeks old, was calm and quiet when Harary was physically present in the same room. Whenever Harary left the room, the kitten would become noisy and restless.

For the experiment, the kitten was placed alone in a wooden box with its floor divided into twenty-four numbered squares. The behavioral measures employed to assess activity were the number of meows per 100 seconds and the number of squares entered into per 100 seconds by the kitten. The kitten was "scored" as entering any square into which it had placed both forepaws.

"Intriguingly," Dr. Ruehl said, "when Harary was placed in one of his experimental rooms and was in the process of undergoing an out-of-body experience, the kitten did not meow once in eight different OBE periods. It was as though Harary's calming spirit had entered the room with the cat. However, during eight control periods when Harary was in an experimental room and *not* undergoing an OBE, the kitten meowed thirty-seven times. Its 'meow rate' was 0 per 100 seconds during OBEs; 3.85 per 100 seconds during controls."

Dr. Ruehl also pointed out that the kitten became extremely inactive during an OBE, averaging only 0.21 squares entered per 100 seconds, as opposed to 3.54 per 100 seconds during a control. "Once again," the physicist noted, "the kitten appeared to have sensed Harary's presence during OBEs."

In another phase of the experiment, Harary was asked to *pretend* he was undergoing an OBE by trying to imagine himself in the room with the kitten, patting it and playing with it. In other words, he would go through the mental motions of having an OBE without actually experiencing one. "Significantly, the kitten was not calmed during the imaginary OBE," Dr. Ruehl explained.

In yet another stage of the investigation, the kitten's orientation relative to Harary's spirit's position in the room was measured. Harary visited four different locations, fifteen feet apart, each near the kitten. "Importantly," Dr. Ruehl emphasized, "the animal displayed a definite shift in position toward Harary's actual OBE locations."

In Dr. Ruehl's opinion, "This dramatic demonstration of a psychic bond between man and cat is all the more impressive when one considers that the kitten was an absolutely objective participant—with no bias whatsoever as to the outcome of the investigation. However, further testing of the kitten became impractical when it became accustomed to the experimental box and the researchers handling it.

"As a fascinating sidebar," Dr. Ruehl added, "it should be noted that many of the human participants also perceived Harary's spirit form when he was projecting his spiritual essence during an OBE. This experiment must be ranked as one of the most impressive experiments in the annals of parapsychology."

Dr. Ruehl went on to share personal experiences of his own with a telepathic cat named Simba.

"I'll never forget my first encounter with him," Dr. Ruehl said. "It was a few years ago when I was a graduate physics student at UCLA. Several of us shared a large office on the second floor of Kinsey Hall. I had just entered the office one autumn morning and placed my briefcase on my desk when I spotted a cat slinking toward me. He wore a coat of thick orange fur to which was attached a long tail ringed with alternating bands of black and orange. I was told that his name was Simba, and he greeted me with a lusty meow.

"I responded to his salutation by stroking his head, tickling him under his chin, and rubbing the sides of his soft body," Dr. Ruehl continued. "Simba acknowledged pleasure at such treatment by purring loudly."

Dr. Ruehl learned that Simba's owner, Ken, another graduate student, had been booted out of his apartment for smuggling a cat into his room. The graduate physics office was serving as a temporary refuge for the fugitive feline. Having some knowledge of cats, Ruehl proceeded to gather some grass and leaves in a cardboard box and put Simba's forepaws in it, moving them back and forth in a scratching motion. The physicist knew that this was the technique that a mother cat uses to teach her kitten how to use a litter box, and it worked like magic for Simba until a formal sandbox was secured for him.

That afternoon, as Ruehl was perusing a physics journal at his desk, he noticed Simba scamper across the room and leap onto the table where the telephone was. The telephone rang a moment later.

"At the time, I did not pay any particular heed to the incident," Ruehl admitted. "But later that same day, Simba again went through a similar acrobatic routine, arriving beside the telephone just before it rang. Another student was in the room at the time, but he had not noticed Simba's mad dash across the room. The thought that Simba might be clairaudient flashed through my brain for the first time."

Two days later, Ruehl was in the office with Ken and an undergraduate who was seeking some assistance with a problem in quantum mechanics. "Suddenly," Ruehl recalled, "Simba bolted over to the phone milliseconds before it began to ring. This time, all three of us witnessed the occurrence. I asked Ken about it, but he swore that he had never seen Simba react in that manner."

During the ensuing week, Ruehl and several others observed Simba's telepathic behavior. Since the graduate students had been alerted to the potential phenomenon involved in Simba's dashes to the telephone, six additional incidents were recorded in a careful, scientific manner.

"I wanted to study Simba's apparent paranormal behavior under controlled conditions," Ruehl said. "But, alas, Ken had found a new apartment where pets were welcome, and he took Simba away from our domain. He told me that he kept a watchful eye on Simba, but he said that the feline never exhibited any precognitive aptitude in the new domicile.

"Could Simba's antics have been purely coincidental with no psychic element whatsoever involved?" Dr. Ruehl asked, putting the query forward for examination. "Or did his behavior represent tangible proof of powers from another dominion?

"To accept the latter hypothesis, we must explain why Simba manifested his telepathic powers only in the second-floor office at Kinsey Hall. One possibility is that he might have been peculiarly sensitive to the vibrational frequency of incoming calls to the office phone, but to no others.

"Alternately," Dr. Ruehl hypothesized, "the specific construction of the office walls and the floor might have somehow amplified those vibrations and brought out Simba's latent psychic powers. While the walls and floor appeared outwardly to be composed of standard materials, perhaps some contaminants were present in sufficient quantity to render him telepathic while there.

"Or, conceivably, some type of psychic link existed between Simba and myself, whereby my presence gave his latent psychic abilities a 'jumpstart,'" the physicist speculated. "As far as I was able to ascertain, Simba exhibited his telephonic prescience only when I was also present in the room with him. While I personally favor this explanation, I can offer no tangible proof of its validity.

"While the enigma of his telepathic ability may never be solved," Dr. Ruehl conceded, "I will always remember my close encounters with a cat named Simba."

What Your Choice of Pet Reveals About Your Personality

Doris Saltan, a San Francisco psychologist, says that the kind of pet that you prefer reveals a great deal about the sort of person you are. According to Ms. Saltan, people project their own desires and values onto their pets. For example, those who like independence will choose an animal that reflects that quality. Men and women who crave affection will select the pet that will permit them to express their feelings of tenderness.

Because a harmonious interaction with the pet one chooses is very important to a meaningful relationship between animal and human, Ms. Saltan says that she often advises people on the type of pet that they should get.

The psychologist comments that the dog has always been considered the most faithful of pets. The dog is also the animal with which the majority of people feel most comfortable.

A person who chooses a cute and affectionate dog from one of the smaller breeds is probably the kind of individual who needs a great deal of cuddling and attention. Such a person, according to Ms. Saltan, is also "sociable and good-hearted."

On the other hand, the kind of person who selects a purebred dog as his animal of preference is "success-oriented and ambitious," who places a heavy emphasis on appearance. He or she also likes to be surrounded by important people who can help in the acquisition of special goals.

"Cat lovers have very complex personalities," observes Ms. Saltan, pointing out that the cat has always been associated with mystery, superstition, and the occult.

"Cat lovers are characterized by attitudes and taste that manifest often for no apparent reason," she says. "People who choose cats as pets are sensual and captivating and have personalities that are fascinating and full of mystery."

The psychologist notes that, generally speaking, people either love cats and idealize them or they loathe them and are afraid of them.

For centuries, birds have graced peoples' homes because of their colorful plumage and the ability of certain species to sing or to mimic human speech.

Ms. Saltan lists three types of people who like birds:

1) Those who buy a bird of beautiful plumage in order to show it off and receive compliments from envious friends.
2) Those artistic folk who love nature and who enjoy songbirds in their homes.
3) The great communicators, who by acquiring parrots and other talking birds thereby reveal a desire to make their opinions known to others.

Among the most admired of animals is the horse. According to Ms. Saltan, "A love of horses for whatever reason reflects a personality that admires strength, pride, and security. This type of person is practical and virtuous."

The San Francisco psychologist goes on to identify those horse owners who seem only to want to look at their animals and pet them, and the horse lovers who seemingly exist only to ride their steed. "For them, nothing is more exciting than riding their favorite horse."

What kind of a person would keep a python in his house?

According to Ms. Saltan, the sort of individual who keeps a reptile for a pet ". . . shows a tendency toward great intelligence and versatility."

The vast majority of people are repulsed or frightened by the very sight of snakes. The reptile lover may be "restless, in search of new sensations, strong emotions, and risks."

In Ms. Saltan's experience, the person who keeps a snake in the house probably ". . . doesn't socialize very much and suffers from contradictory emotions when it comes to love."

Ms. Saltan says that certain people choose fish for pets for two reasons: "Because they're easy to care for or because they feel an affinity toward them."

Those individuals who feel an affinity or identification with fish are quite likely to be introverted. They would rather watch colorful fish swimming in their home aquariums than participate in the stress and chaos that constitute modern life.

Devoted fish people tend to fantasize, Ms. Saltan said: "They are imaginative, like vivid colors, and often have trouble distinguishing between fantasy and reality."

While most people are repulsed by the very idea of keeping rodents as pets, Ms. Saltan states that those animal lovers who fancy mice "are sweet and sensitive."

Continuing her point, the psychologist says that "mouse lovers" are very often those people who ". . . have a desire to help those weaker than themselves." They also serve as peacemakers, because they personally cannot stand arguments.

Folks who choose squirrels as their significant pet are really yearning for their own freedom, Ms. Saltan said. "They also are quick to react, because they have agile, active minds."

How Much Do You Love *Your* Pet?

As we explore the mysterious bond that melds pets and their owners together, we cannot ignore the extreme lengths that some people will go to express their love and devotion to their favorite animal.

Recently wed Josephine and Stewart McSkimming choose to live forty miles apart in separate houses because they discovered their two female dogs hate each other. Both of the newlyweds raised their dogs from pups, and neither can bear to be separated from his or her animal. The McSkimmings have resigned themselves to a marriage at a distance until one of the pets dies.

The couple had married with the intention of living in 56-year-old Stewart's home in New Galloway, Scotland, but then they found that Josephine's Labrador, Tanya, and Stewart's springer spaniel, Gale, seemed determined to maul each other in endless scrappy skirmishes.

Josephine, a 43-year-old artist, stated that she and Stewart had even ended up in the hospital with dog bites when they attempted to separate the dogs during one particularly pitched battle.

The best the couple can do at the present time is to travel to each other's homes three or four times a week. Gale sleeps in Stewart's car, while Tanya stays in Josephine's van during the couple's conjugal visits.

*   *   *

Certainly, the McSkimmings are displaying an incredible kind of devotion to their dogs in that they are sacrificing their own marital bliss for the sake of their animals' peace of mind. But psychologist Elayne Kahn, author of several books, including *Love Codes*, recently told journalist Paulette Cooper that many women actually love their pets more than they love their husbands.

Dr. Kahn repeated the story of one of her patients who got a divorce because of her great love for her cat. It seems that her husband developed an allergic reaction to the feline and delivered the ultimatum that either he or the cat would have to go. The woman chose her cat.

The psychologist went on to point out that some women will remain in an unhappy marriage because they cannot bear to leave their pet.

"It's harder to get visitation rights to a pet than it is to children," Dr. Kahn said.

In some cases, women have complained to Dr. Kahn that their pets are more appreciative than their husbands. A dog may be thankful for a biscuit, but a husband demands much more than that.

Women have also told the psychologist that they can talk more easily to their pets than to their husbands. "I think ninety-five percent of people confide in their pets," she said.

Billy Thomas of Wakefield, England, is another husband who may regret delivering the "it's the cat or me" ultimatum. On the other hand, in Thomas's case, he had to deal with 129 cats!

When Thomas talked to the press in December, 1991, the couple had not yet divorced; but Billy, a gardener, was insisting that their separation had come about as a direct result of his wife Christine's preference for the company of her dozens of cats to his.

The huge bills for food and veterinary visits for the cat commune caused the Thomases great financial distress. However, even without a husband and with very little money, the 42-year-old Christine vowed that she would not abandon her felines. She admitted that she was very unhappy when Billy, 48, moved out, but she cannot forsake her furry friends.

Christine, a former psychiatric nurse, began caring for cats as a kind of hobby when a back injury in 1974 left her unable to walk. What began as a few kitties around the house greatly increased as her health returned.

When it reached the point where thirty meowing cats shared their two-bedroom home and another ninety-nine felines snuggled together in heated sheds in the backyard, Billy Thomas delivered his ultimatum.

"The only way Billy will come back is if the cats are gone," Christine told journalist Steve Plamann. "And I can't take him back under those circumstances."

One of the most bizarre custody cases on record in American courtrooms took place on September 5, 1990, when Linda Walker of Novi, Michigan, won custody of fourteen-foot-long Samson and four-foot-long Jake, her beloved pythons.

"These guys are my babies," Ms. Walker told writer Susan Fenton. "I love them as much as any parent loves her kids."

Linda Walker, 42, had originally won custody of both babies in July, but she asked her ex-husband Terry to keep the mighty Samson until she could find a house.

When, a few weeks later in August, a local newspaper carried an article detailing how Samson had almost been run over by a car while being taken for a "walk" by her ex-husband, an outraged Linda demanded the immediate return of the fourteen-foot python. But this time Terry was claiming that possession was nine-tenths of the law, and he refused to return his ex-wife's baby.

Fortunately for Ms. Walker, County Judge Gene Schnelz, who had originally granted Ms. Walker full custody of her "children," once again decreed that she should receive custody of both pythons.

While it is true that some marriages and relationships may break up over pets, we are certain that there are even more unions that are more profoundly cemented because of a mutual love for animals.

At the recent wedding of Kimberly Simmons and Paul Norton in an outdoor ceremony at a public park in Hamilton, New Jersey, two of the flower girls and the ring bearer were dogs. All three of the dogs were whippets, and they were all extravagantly attired.

Duke, the ring bearer, was outfitted in a gray doggie tuxedo with a pink ruffle on his shirt. The flower girls, Cameo and Knee-Hi, wore white lace gowns.

Kimberly, a Princeton, New Jersey, dog groomer, was the proud owner of the three classy whippets.

"My dogs are like my children," Kimberly, 23, told writer Peter Fenton. "There was no way that I could have left them home during this most special moment of my life."

Since Duke, Cameo, and Knee-Hi were all show dogs and accustomed to being on their best behavior, there were no embarrassing incidents during the ceremony.

And what about the groom? Will he soon be delivering an ultimatum that it's either him or the dogs?

Paul Norton said that he had grown to love the dogs in the three years that he had dated Kimberly. "I was completely open to having them take part in our wedding," he said.

Then there's Lee Day, a dog groomer from Bloomfield, New Jersey, who is more than delighted to arrange marriages, baptisms, bar mitzvahs, and other religious rites for dogs.

Ms. Day was the person who staged the lavish ceremony for Tammy Faye Bakker's Yorkshire terrier Corky when the Bakkers were still in control of their Praise the Lord empire. She performed the televised ceremony that united Corky and a white poodle named Peaches in the Christian marriage rite. Each of the canines wore elegant formal wedding attire, and the ceremony was witnessed by the massive PTL network audience.

Lee Day has conducted marriage rites for pets on "The Morton Downey, Jr. Show," "A Current Affair," and "The Regis Philbin Show." When she pronounces a couple linked in marriage, she decrees that they are joined for as long as they both shall "lick." Wedding rings would be impractical, so she seals their vows with an exchange of gold-plated collars.

Do you love your cat enough to buy your furry friend a special $19.95 video for felines?

Steve Malarkey has created a unique tape called *Video Catnip*, a thirty-minute nature film that enchants cats by showing them tantalizing footage of real birds, squirrels, and chipmunks gamboling across the screen. Satisfied customers have already bought thousands of the videos, and more than three hundred pet stores carry *Video Catnip*.

Although some cat owners express tongue-in-cheek concern over their pet becoming a "couch potato," most agree that their cat is mesmerized by the images of the animals on the screen. Numerous customers have expressed surprise over their feline's fascination with the film. Prior to exposure to *Video Catnip*, many cats paid absolutely no attention to the moving pictures on the television set. Malarkey claims that his video holds the interest of 90 percent of adult indoor cats.

Brian and Anita Blazer would quite likely buy a copy of *Video Catnip* for their cat—if they had one. The Blazers, who reside in Heflin, Alabama, favor more exotic pets, but they would probably put in their order to Steve Malarkey for special videos for their baboon, their African monkey, their two miniature Vietnamese pot-bellied pigs, their giant South American rodent, their Burmese mountain tortoise, their mammoth toad, their python—and for all of their other assorted lizards, scorpions, and cockroaches. The Blazers love their animals enough to have turned their home completely over to their merry menagerie, and they live in a two-bedroom home as one big happy family.

The Blazers have no human children, but Kenya, the baboon, wears diapers, which Anita changes about every two hours. The sometimes hectic activity in the home makes it seem as though there's a houseful of kids running around.

Anita, 35, said that most of the time the animals are quite well behaved. The potbellied pigs are housebroken, and they let the Blazers know when they need to go outside to obey the call of nature. The rest of the critters don't make too much of a mess, and the Blazers keep cedar shavings in the cages to help absorb the odors.

Brian once managed a zoo in North Carolina for seven years; and he and Anita load up the animals four days a week to visit various elementary and high schools in the area, thus enriching the students' knowledge of geography, ecology, biology, and wildlife protection.

Do you love your dog enough to plunge into raging floodwaters to save its life?

Twenty-one-year-old Gina Erdman, a student from Albuquerque, New Mexico, only took the time required to whisper a little prayer for divine assistance before she jumped into a raging cascade of water to save her two-year-old female pup, Sammy.

Sammy had been romping playfully in a shallow flood-control ditch when a torrent of rainwater from a recent storm began cascading down from the nearby Sandia Mountains. In moments, the slow trickle of water in the ditch was transformed into a roaring river.

As Gina watched in terror, Sammy was swept away. Although her mind registered that it would be suicide to jump into the ditch, her heart told her that she must try to save her pup.

By what she would later term "sheer instinct," Gina plunged into the fast-moving water, managing somehow to catch up to Sammy and grab hold of her fur. Although the current in the ditch was building up a tremendous pull, the water level was still shallow enough for Gina to be able to stand and to walk with her dog to the edge of the ditch.

Then another wall of water roared into the flood-control ditch, crashed down upon them, and knocked Gina off her feet. At speeds later estimated to be at least twenty miles an hour, she and Sammy were swept down the gully. Gina had to fight the unyielding current in order to avoid being battered into unconsciousness by concrete and steel supports.

As Gina was being buffeted black and blue, she beheld an irony that was almost too bitter to accept. From time to time, Sammy would leave her, scamper up out of the water onto the bank, then jump back in the ditch and swim back to her side.

Sammy didn't need to be rescued at all. But now Gina certainly did!

She wondered if this was her time to die. "I was swept under streets, through parks, and alongside backyards," she told writer Joe Cassidy for the November 20, 1990, issue of *Globe*. "I could see people barbecueing and relaxing in lounge chairs. There was shock on their faces as they saw me shooting past."

Gina will be eternally grateful that firefighters pulled her to safety when they did. She was completely exhausted and about to lose consciousness. Sammy bounded out of the water on her own.

The doctors removed stones and bits of concrete that had become embedded in her skin, but Gina suffered no permanent injuries. Sammy wasn't hurt at all.

Do you cherish your dog enough to administer the "kiss of life," mouth-to-mouth resuscitation, if your pet were choking to death? Patrolman John Bassler, an assistant trainer in Pittsburgh's K-9 school, didn't bother to think twice before he used the method to save his dog Heidi's life.

Bassler was at home one night in the fall of 1991 when Heidi came running to him with a tennis ball lodged in her throat. By the time that he had removed the object, his beloved pet had stopped breathing. Her eyes were glazed over, and her tongue was extended, swollen, and purplish in color. He could detect no heartbeat.

Patrolman Bassler held Heidi's mouth shut, put his mouth over her nose, then gave her three good breaths.

He felt Heidi's chest rise and expand. He knelt beside her, then gave her three chest compressions.

"I saw her eyes blink," he said. "In a couple of minutes, she was fine."

Ernie Tomasko, Bassler's chief at the K-9 academy, commended his assistant. Many people won't do CPR to save another human being, Tomasko observed wryly, to say nothing of performing the "kiss of life" on an animal. "Obviously," Tomasko said, "John Bassler loves his dog very much."

All right. Perhaps you would give the kiss of life to your favorite dog or cat, but how many of you can honestly say that you would perform the life-bestowing act on a pet rattlesnake? Zookeeper Mark O'Shea continued to breathe into the throat of a deadly diamondback rattler for five and a half hours until he had restored it to life.

O'Shea, a thirty-year-old expert on snakes for a popular safari park in England, was horrified to find that the rattlesnake was being swallowed by its cagemate, a giant California king snake. The zookeeper yanked the half-swallowed rattler free, but found that its heart had stopped.

The quick-thinking O'Shea put a tube down the snake's throat and began practicing the breath of life. It took him five and a half hours of steady effort, but his persistence was rewarded when he at last brought the rattler back to consciousness.

The exhausted but delighted O'Shea named the snake Lazarus— and saw to it that from that time on the rattler had its own cage.

Establishing a Mind Linkup with Your Pet

When Brad Steiger was a boy of thirteen, he had a pet cat with whom he had established a remarkable mind linkup. Physically there was certainly nothing unusual about the feline—except that a mischievous mixture of genes had swirled the color pattern that Mother Nature intended as regular orange tiger stripes into peculiarly placed splotches. Because of the unsymmetrical splashes of orange indiscriminately shaded with black, the cat appeared to have a grotesquely human face. With all the directness of a thirteen-year-old, Brad had studied the tiny gargoyle-like face and named the animal Demonpuss, Demon for short.

Wherever Brad went, the cat would seem to materialize in an almost magical way. If he were feeding the pigs or the cattle on the Iowa farm on which he was reared, the cat would leap from the low roof of a nearby livestock shed onto Brad's shoulders. There, balancing herself without piercing the boy's flesh with her claws, Demon would ride like a parrot on the shoulder of a seaman. In winter months, when Brad wore a thick wool coat against the harsh prairie cold, Demon would feel free to sink in her claws as far as necessary to maintain her balance.

Whether Brad was feeding the cattle, picking eggs in the henhouse, or currying his pet calves, Demon sat on his shoulder, quietly seeming to inspect the quality of his work.

When Brad's father decided to limit the number of hogs to be raised on their farm, a small pig house in very good condition was left vacant. The building was hauled to a pleasant spot in a grove of pine trees where Brad's nine-year-old sister June was given half of the area for her playhouse, and Brad was given the other half for his art studio.

As a teenager, Brad's greatest pleasure lay in writing stories and illustrating them. Whenever he had the briefest spare moment from baling hay, unloading corn, doing the livestock chores, or working in the fields, he would dash to his studio and work at his art.

He was never at his drawing board for longer than five minutes before Demon would jump through the open window and sit quietly on her haunches beside him. She would never play with the art gum eraser or the pencils. She would not clean herself or stretch out for a nap. She would sit there in rapt attention and watch Brad draw.

Because of the erratic schedule of farmwork during the daytime, there was never anything approaching set times when Brad might rush to his drawing board for a few minutes of artistic expression before he went back to his appointed duties. It would have been impossible for the cat to establish a habit pattern conditioned by the regularity of her master's routine. Brad's appearances at his little studio were totally spontaneous and completely at random.

The evening's schedule was no more consistent. One day's work might demand unloading bales of hay until long after dark. A rainy day meant early quitting time and an opportunity to begin drawing right after supper. Then there were the nights that Brad's father played catcher on the town's softball team, and Brad played right field on the junior team.

The fact that Demon would appear within minutes of Brad's settling himself at his drawing board—regardless of the time, day or night—convinced the teenaged boy that he and his pet cat had established a special kind of mind attunement. Significant for the boy's psychological development was the animal's apparent desire to be with him. A cat, traditionally noted for its aloofness and independence, actually wanted to be with him.

Brad came to realize that any life form treated with kindness, love, and respect would return that positive energy many times over—and that there is a beautiful Oneness to all of life.

In 1972, Brad, now an established author in the metaphysical and paranormal fields, was asked to review a book by a young woman who had developed mediumistic abilities and had written about her contact with a spirit entity named Seth. The book became the classic *Seth Speaks: The Eternal Validity of the Soul*, and the medium was, of course, Jane Roberts.

In a later work, *The "Unknown" Reality: A Seth Book*, the multidimensional entity known as Seth asserted that animals as we know them today are neither superior nor inferior to the human species. Animals are simply one form that consciousness has taken in its multitudinous expression, while we humans constitute another such form.

According to Seth, the totem pole displayed by the American Indians of the Northwest is a remnant of a time in which there was much greater communication between the human and the animal species. In those days, people went directly to the animals to learn, and it was from them that humankind acquired the knowledge of various medicinal herbs.

Although many sensitive men and women are distressed by the apparent cruelty that certain animals exhibit toward one another, Jane channeled Seth's observation of the two linked characteristics of animal consciousness—*i.e.*, a sense of justice and a biological compassion "understood at the deepest cellular levels."

In *The Nature of Personal Reality*, Seth illustrates his point by stressing that a cat killing and eating a mouse is not evil: "On biological levels, both animals understand. The consciousness of the mouse, under the innate knowledge of impending pain, leaves its body. The cat uses the warm flesh. The mouse itself has been both hunter as well as prey. . . . At certain levels both cat and mouse understand the nature of the life energy that they share, and are not—in those terms—jealous for their own individuality . . . they have a built-in unconscious sense of unity with nature in which they know they will not be lost or immersed."

Constantly stressing the truth that both animal and human consciousness have intrinsic value, Seth strongly opposes the processes of learning more about animals by killing or dissecting them. The better way, the spirit entity counseled, was to identify with the animal that we wish to study.

"There are ways of identifying with animals. . . . There are ways of learning *from* animals," Seth states firmly in *The "Unknown" Reality*. "If you did not feel any need to destroy reality (in your terms) in order to understand it, then you would not need to dissect animals, hoping to discover the reasons for human diseases. You would have attained a living knowledge long ago, in which diseases as such did not occur. You would have understood long ago the connections between mind and body, feelings and health, and illness."

* * *

Clarisa Bernhardt, one of North America's leading psychic-sensitives, has long established a remarkable telepathic connection with animals.

Not long ago she was involved in a case in which she assisted the authorities in locating a missing woman. After she had completed providing her psychic impressions of the woman's whereabouts, one of the police officials invited her to dinner at his house.

As Clarisa was sitting quietly on a sofa awaiting the serving of the evening meal, her host's Siamese cat approached her and laid a gentle paw on her ankle.

Clarisa smiled and asked the cat how she was. The answer came in a telepathic image in the psychic-sensitive's mind. The cat was clearly projecting an image of a yellow square, accompanied by a slight sensation of urgency and desire.

"Do you occasionally give your cat a pat of butter?" Clarisa asked the police official's wife.

"Why, yes," the woman answered, smiling her astonishment at Clarisa's query. "It happens to be her favorite treat."

"Well," Clarisa informed her, "she just asked me to tell you that she would like another pat of butter right away."

Recently, when Clarisa and her husband were vacationing in Arizona's beautiful redrock country near Sedona, they stayed at a resort about a mile from the legendary Bell Rock. She had noticed a friendly "wolf-tiger" cat lurking about the resort area, and she learned that the animal belonged to a couple staying in a condominium not far from them.

One day as Clarisa was resting in the master bedroom, the neighborly cat jumped in through an open window. Completely ignoring her physical presence, the tiger cat crawled under the bed as if he owned the place.

In a few moments, the bold visitor re-emerged and telepathically demanded of Clarisa: "Where are the tuna fish sandwiches?"

Clarisa laughed and formed the thought in her own mind: "There are no tuna fish sandwiches under our bed."

With an air of disappointment bordering on disgust, the cat stared at Clarisa for a few seconds, then bounded out of the bedroom and vanished into the wooded area surrounding the resort.

Later that day, Clarisa encountered the cat's owners while on a nature walk in the area. "Do you keep tuna fish sandwiches under your bed for your cat?" she asked them.

The couple burst out laughing. "Yes, it's a game we play with Rasputin. But how could you possibly know that?"

"Rasputin told me," Clarisa answered them, thereby provoking even greater roars of laughter.

On Labor Day a few years ago, Clarisa was asked by a San Jose, California, private investigator to assist him on a grim case of a missing woman and her baby.

As they entered the home of the missing mother and child, a magnificent German shepherd approached Clarisa. "He knew that I was there to help," she said.

"He telepathically projected the image of an old rusty orange pickup and the description of a man who had forced his way into the home. He must have known the intruder, for he also gave me a vision of a half-mile area in which the pickup could be found."

Clarisa sadly commented that the story did not have a happy ending. The woman and her child had been murdered by the man who had abducted them.

"But neighbors remembered having seen an old rusty orange pickup in the neighborhood on the day the two victims disappeared," she stated. "The vehicle was found in the vicinity that the dog described to me, and the owner of the pickup fit the description of the intruder that the German shepherd had telepathically projected. Consequently, the man was brought to trial and was sentenced for the deaths of the woman and her baby."

As an afterword on that case, Clarisa remembered that as she and the private investigator were leaving the home after her revealing conversation with the German shepherd, a Siamese cat ran up to her and asked, "Please help my paw."

While the puzzled investigator stood by, Clarisa bandaged the cat's paw with her handkerchief.

"The universe is all tied together," she told the man when he asked how she was able to talk to animals.

Exercises To Establish Telepathic Communication with Your Pet

Here is a very simple exercise to help you develop a closer telepathic bond with your pet.

Telepathy is an ability which we all have and which is quite easy to trigger. All you need to do to make contact with your pets is to think intently of them and form a mental image of what you wish to communicate.

Think of the mind as a vast reservoir of energy ready to be released into the unknown. Form the image in your mind, then let go of it and visualize it floating into your pet's brain.

As a gauge of your success in this exercise, you should set a time limit on your thought projection, then note how long it takes to get a positive feedback or response.

You might start by mentally asking your pet to come to you when you are in different rooms of the house or in different outdoor areas. Keep projecting the thought until your pet responds to the unspoken command.

On another occasion, wait until your pet has its back turned toward you and is comfortably relaxing or focusing on some other activity. Begin to concentrate on the back of the animal's head.

Imagine that there is a stream of light flowing from your eyes. Then imagine that on that stream of light you are sending the message, "Turn around and look at me."

Don't be discouraged if your pet does not turn around and look at you immediately. Just keep at it, and within a few minutes your pet will turn and stare directly at you.

The following experiment is a bit more difficult, but you may wish to attempt it after you and your pet have mastered the two simpler exercises. Many people we know have achieved remarkable results by following these instructions:

Seat yourself at a table, brightly lighted by a lamp placed somewhat behind you and shining directly on a piece of paper in front of you.

Your face should be turned toward the spot where your pet is seated or reclining, some distance away, with its back to you.

On the piece of paper before you, draw a simple line sketch of an object that would be familiar to your pet, such as a ball, a rubber bone, a favorite toy. After drawing the figure, focus your attention upon it. Concentrate on it for a minute.

Then, mentally, *will* your pet to receive the impression that you are transmitting. Concentrate on this transmission of image for another minute.

Next, take three comfortably deep breaths, then transmit a verbal command that your pet should fetch or direct its attention to the object that you have drawn. For example, "Bring me the ball"; "Fetch the bone."

Continue sending the verbal command for at least another minute.

You should never keep at this exercise until you are weary of it or bored. You must always maintain a fresh, enthusiastic attitude for best results.

After some practice, the results you will achieve will be quite dramatic, and you will have progressed much farther toward establishing a powerful telepathic linkup with your pet.

No part of any of the above exercises should be forced. It is important to remain relaxed. Then, when you achieve positive results, use them to fix the knowledge in your mind that telepathy between you and your pet really works.

Part Two

THE LIFESAVERS, THE DEFENDERS, AND THE CRIMEBUSTERS

Nicolo the Defender

Michael Talbot, author of the brilliant book *The Holographic Universe*, which uses the latest theories in physics to explain the paranormal activities of the mind, told us of the extraordinary circumstances during which his cat Nicolo became his courageous defender.

A few years ago, Michael, who has also written a study of reincarnation, was having a telephone "reading" from Jim Gordon, a well-known psychic from Hawaii. During the course of their conversation, Michael asked Gordon if animals had past lives.

The psychic-sensitive answered in the affirmative.

"Well," Talbot wanted to know, "what about my two cats, Ugo and Nicolo?"

Gordon replied that Ugo, gentle and loving, tried always to incarnate in homes in which the owner played the piano. Ugo was fascinated by music and was especially thrilled by the sound of a piano.

Michael found this interesting, since he played the piano as a hobby, and he had noticed Ugo's delight when he sat down at the keyboard.

What about Nicolo?

Gordon told Michael that his Nicky was a much older soul and had experienced many incarnations. The psychic-sensitive stated that Nicky was interested in profound things far more than matters of day-to-day survival.

Talbot reflected how Nicky seemed to enjoy watching him write. It sometimes seemed as if the cat were somehow entering into a full understanding of the creative process.

Gordon went on to state that Nicolo had once been a zebra, then a lion and a tiger. He had continually been moving upward on the spiritual evolutionary scale to the point where he was now beginning to question his cathood.

The psychic-sensitive said that Nicky had also been a Tibetan temple guardian cat in a former existence. Michael was aware of there having been Egyptian temple guardian cats, but he was uncertain if the Tibetans ever employed felines in such a manner.

"The bottom line," Michael said, "was that Nicky had come to me to be my defender, my protector. I actually found this quite amusing, because Nicky was a total love rag. He loved people, and everyone loved him. He seemed the least likely protector imaginable."

Then one night Michael was awakened by a tremendous crash in his apartment.

"I got out of bed and confronted a man standing in the hallway. He had a gun in his hand and he ordered me to get the hell back into my bedroom."

Michael saw that he had no choice other than to comply immediately with the robber's command.

"Just then, Nicky shot past me like a bullet, hissing, howling, growling," Michael said. "The love rag had been transformed into this incredible raging monster. To my amazement, Nicky attacked the burglar—gun and all—with such fury that the man left in panic by the front door!"

Later, when Michael examined his apartment, he discovered that the burglar's point of entry had been at a window—where he had bent the grates designed to keep out thieves.

"The burglar had been so terrified of my little Nicky that he hadn't even bothered to try to escape via the route by which he had broken into my apartment," Michael said. "The front door was the fastest point of departure from my courageous and savage little defender.

"Whether you accept the concept of reincarnation or not, Nicolo had certainly proved himself to be my defender."

Katrina Is Named "Animal of the Year" for Defending Blind Owner

Although Diane Motchuk's gentle yellow Labrador guide dog Katrina had never been in a fight in her life, she bravely defended her thirty-five-year-old owner from the vicious attack of a pit bull.

Diane, a volunteer social worker, was walking home after a shopping trip in the Toronto suburb of York in May, 1989. She was holding Katrina's halter when her sensitive hearing picked up the sound of a dog's paws running toward them.

She felt Katrina jump into the air, and she heard a loud thudding collision. Diane frantically concluded that something must have struck her faithful guide dog.

Then she heard the distressing sounds of yelping, barking, growling, the snapping of dogs' jaws opening and closing. People were screaming and running toward them.

This new ruckus told Diane that for some unfathomable reason, another dog had attacked Katrina. She wanted to help her friend, but she didn't know what to do. Finally, in desperation, she simply jumped down on the struggling dogs.

Diane was horror-struck as she found the attacker's head and felt its sharp teeth deeply imbedded in Katrina's neck. She exerted all of her strength in an attempt to pry the cruel jaws loose from her dog's flesh, but they were as firmly set as a steel clamp.

After what seemed an eternity of violence and terror, the other dog's owner came running upon the scene and began to beat both animals. When the dogs were parted, he put a leash on his undisciplined brute and dragged it away.

"I knelt down beside Katrina and felt her courageously try to stand," Diane Motchuk told reporter Esmond Choueke. "I held her head in my arms and I could feel her blood all over me. 'Katrina,' I said, 'I love you very much. You saved my life.'"

Witnesses to the attack then provided Diane with the complete story. For no reason that anyone could ascertain, a pit bull suddenly began running toward the blind woman and her guide dog. Without any sign of provocation from either Ms. Motchuk or Katrina, the pit bull launched a savage attack that was intercepted by the gentle Labrador. It appeared, according to some who observed the pit bull's vicious lunge at Ms. Motchuk, that the brutish animal simply wished to kill someone.

It required nearly one hundred stitches to repair Katrina's ripped and torn flesh, but it was not long before she was back at Diane Motchuk's side.

York Animal Control Officer George Banton stated that Katrina had won everyone's heart ". . . for being such a loving, fearless pet in offering her own life to defend her mistress from serious injury or death." Officer Banton went on to emphasize that Katrina's act of valor was especially laudatory because she was a very gentle animal that had never before been in a fight.

On September 18, 1989, in a special ceremony at York City Hall, Mayor Fergy Brown placed a medallion around Katrina's neck that proclaimed her Animal of the Year.

Eve the Rottweiler Rescues Paralyzed Owner from Fiery Truck

It started out as a very pleasant excursion for Kathie Vaughan and her six-year-old pet Rottweiler, Eve. They left Indianapolis that winter's day in 1991 to drive to an antique dealers show in Atlanta.

They were only a few miles from home when the nightmare began. Forty-one-year-old Kathie heard a strange "pop"—and the steering wheel was almost yanked out of her hands.

Although for six years she had been paralyzed from the waist down with multiple sclerosis, Kathie had maintained excellent upper body strength. She struggled to regain control of the fishtailing truck, and she managed at last to bring it to a screeching stop.

What could be wrong? She had just bought the used truck earlier that day—for the trip to Atlanta.

Then, to her horror, she saw that the cab was filling with foul-smelling black smoke. The truck was on fire! It could within moments burst into a fireball that would consume both Eve and herself.

"I shouted at Eve, 'We've gotta get out!' " Kathie Vaughan wrote of her narrow escape in the January 28, 1992, issue of *The Examiner.* "Then I shoved her out the door, grabbed the frame of my wheelchair, and flung it after her."

The horror intensified when Kathie, coughing and choking because of the dense smoke, could not find the wheels to her chair. Frantically, her fingers searched for the wheels, but the noxious fumes had disoriented her. The only consistent thought that remained focused in her brain was that the truck was about to explode with her in it.

Kathie had expected Eve to run from the fire, to retreat to safety. But now she was aware of the big dog trying to grab her arm with her teeth. Kathie could hardly breathe, and as her vision was fading, her fear was becoming overwhelming.

"Incredibly, at that instant, Eve yanked my right leg, and I flew out the passenger side of the cab feet first and blacked out," Kathie said.

As she flickered into consciousness, she was dimly aware of Eve's jaws clamped around her ankle, dragging her from the truck.

The 104-pound Rottweiler had scarcely pulled her owner ten feet away from the burning truck when they were rocked by a sickening explosion. Flames swallowed the cab, then leaped eight feet into the air.

Undistracted from the task at hand, Eve continued dragging Kathie to the more complete safety of a nearby ditch. It wasn't until the dog released her ankle that Kathie had regained enough consciousness to realize what a brave thing Eve had done.

"Eve had outdone the most daring deeds of the dogs that I had seen in the movies. She had fearlessly pulled me to safety at the risk of her own life."

But the nerve-wrenching drama was not yet concluded. As Kathie was becoming more aware of the pain in her head and ribs, a police car arrived and an officer attempted to run to her assistance.

Eve, now hypersensitive to all the chaos and danger around them, refused to drop her protective stance and permit the officer to approach them.

"You've got to get farther away!" the policeman yelled at Kathie. "The gas tank can go at any second!"

Startled by the awareness of the new danger and challenge, Kathie began desperately to pull herself toward the police car.

Eve took only a moment to assess the situation, then, seeming to comprehend fully her owner's goal, she offered Kathie her collar and dragged her an additional forty feet to safety.

Kathie stated that it took cautious firemen quite some time to extinguish the burning truck. Perhaps due to their efforts—or a generous quirk of fate—the gas tank never did explode.

As the excitement was abating at last, Eve permitted the officer to approach her and to pet her. "You are an awfully good dog," he told Eve.

Kathie's amused comment was that the pronouncement of "awfully good dog" to summarize the Rottweiler's remarkable acts of courage had her nomination as the understatement of the year.

Bernard the St. Bernard Saves Two Teens from Auto Wreck

Bev and Bill Ray, who live near Eagle, Canada, heard the terrible sounds of the crash from their home. A van careened over a cliff after the driver had failed to negotiate a sharp turn. Within moments, they could hear people screaming for help.

Their eighteen-month-old St. Bernard, named Bernard, could not stand to hear the cries of pain and distress. He threw the full power of his 120 pounds against the chain that bound him to a tree in the Rays' yard and snapped a link, setting himself free. Before either of his owners could utter a command to wait for them, Bernard was bounding over the cliff and down to the van.

Jackie Grover, 16, was still inside the vehicle and unconscious when Bernard squeezed his bulk through the broken windshield's jagged daggers of glass.

"I woke up to find this big dog licking my face," Jackie said. But she couldn't move because her back was broken.

Bernard gently edged her shoulder between his jaws and slowly, carefully pulled her out of the van.

Fifteen-year-old Kate Kirkey had sustained a nasty knock on the head and several serious injuries, but she had managed to crawl out of the smashed van on her own. Once outside, however, she collapsed on the road and began to weep.

Hearing her cries, Bernard came over to Kate and lay down beside her. "I had seen this big dog go inside the van and pull Jackie out," Kate said. "Now he lay beside me and licked my face. Next he put his big head on my shoulder, trying to comfort me. Just his very presence calmed me and helped me a lot."

When Bill and Bev Ray arrived on the scene, they were proud of what Bernard had already accomplished. But then they were startled to discover that their heroic dog had injured himself badly when he had squirmed through the hole in the shattered windshield. A shard of glass had gashed his leg all the way to the bone.

The teenaged girls said that they would never forget what the wonderful Bernard had done for them. "He was so filled with love and compassion," Jackie said. "I will never forget what he did."

Bernard's act of selfless heroism, ignoring his own severe injury, did not surprise Bev and Bill Ray. Bev pointed out that Bernard even carried her grocery bags into the house for her. "And if we're ever hurt, he'll come over and lick us, as if he is trying to heal us. It is easy to see why his breed is so famous for its rescue abilities."

German Shepherd Shoots Her Master—Then Saves His Life

Since his family was away for a few hours on that pleasant summer evening in 1991, marksman Joseph Petrowski thought it would be a perfect time to strip the stock and trigger guard from his rifle, clean it, and adjust the sight. Since he lived in rural St. Laurent, Manitoba, Canada, there were no nearby neighbors to complain about his target shooting.

Petrowski placed the .22 rifle in barrel and clamp form, and tested it several times on a target. After a final shot he reloaded the rifle, then walked in front of the barrel to check the firing pattern on the target.

He knew, of course, that it was a foolish thing to stand in front of a loaded gun; but after all, he was home alone with only his German shepherd Vegas. What could go wrong? He would examine the effects his bullets had on the target, then he would return to the only really safe position when one is shooting—behind the rifle, not in front of it.

When Petrowski heard the small, metallic click, he had but the tiniest fraction of a second to wish that he had not removed the trigger guard from his rifle.

Then he felt the bullet strike and tear into his flesh. He pitched forward on his face and blacked out.

When he regained consciousness, Vegas was pawing at his face and licking him.

Instinctively, Petrowski grabbed her collar, and the powerful dog dragged him over one hundred feet to the deck by the front door of their home.

Before he fainted from loss of blood, pain, and shock, the wounded man managed to crawl to the telephone and tell the operator that he needed help.

When the Mounties found him, Petrowski still had his hand on the phone. At first the officers thought the man was dead, but Petrowski remained conscious of everything that was happening around him.

Later he would remember when he heard a paramedic say that he had lost his heartbeat. Petrowski told himself that it was not his time to die—and he willed his heart to start again.

Once in the hospital, a team of surgeons worked desperately for several hours to save the dying man's life. It was discovered that the bullet had fractured four ribs and ripped up his liver and intestines.

Days afterward, as Petrowski was recuperating from his near-fatal misadventure, someone asked him if he was going to get rid of the dog that had nearly killed him.

Joseph Petrowski was astonished at the question. He had mentally reconstructed the accident and concluded that Vegas had probably brushed against the guardless trigger and the rifle had gone off.

"Vegas didn't do anything wrong," he retorted. "I made a serious mistake when I put myself in front of a loaded rifle. If Vegas hadn't dragged me back to the house, I would have bled to death. She saved my life!"

Hero Dog Fishes Boy from Tidal Pool

What had begun as a pleasant family outing and a picnic at the beach would have been transformed into a horrible tragedy if it had not been for Tess, a brave black Labrador.

Heather Hodder, Tess's owner, was enjoying a beach walk on a summer's day in July 1991, allowing the black Labrador to romp freely along the shore. Suddenly, Tess broke into a run and began to bark wildly at something in a tidal pool just beyond Heather's range of sight.

"The next thing I knew," Heather said, "was that Tess dove straight into that pool. I was concerned, because I knew the tidal pools were quite deep in that part of the shore."

When Heather arrived at the rim of the pool, she was shocked to see a small body floating facedown in the deep water. "Then I realized that Tess had hold of the little body, and she was dragging him out by his trousers. That's when I began furiously to scream for help!"

Heather's screams were heard by the boy's parents, Dean and Cherie Wines, and by his uncle, Clive Oram, who were still enjoying their picnic in some nearby sand dunes. "My God!" Cherie gasped, her mother instinct suddenly activated by the woman's cries for help. "Where is Arron?"

Dean and Clive set out on a run. "I came around a rock and just fifteen yards away saw the dog pulling Arron out of the pool. His lips were blue, and he wasn't breathing."

Dean tried his best to give his son mouth-to-mouth resuscitation, but he knew that he himself was entering into shock. "I'm panicking, man," he told his brother-in-law. "I can't do it!"

Clive calmly moved Dean aside and assumed a kneeling position beside the body of his nephew. Fortunately for two-year-old Arron, his uncle remained cool and brought him back sputtering with the kiss of life.

"That dog is a hero," Cherie told Heather. "She saved our little boy's life!"

Clive and Dean agreed that Arron would have died had Tess not dragged him out of the tidal pool to safety.

As Arron was recovering from his ordeal in a hospital, Dean Wines, a production worker from Ebbe Vale, Wales, reiterated his praise for Tess: "There is no doubt that my son would be dead if it wasn't for that heroic dog. Tess was wonderful, and I can't thank her enough."

Brave Cat Saves Toddler from Rattlesnake in California Home

Holly Lenz of Laguna Niguel, California, was enjoying a quiet October afternoon in the fall of 1990. She had put her two-year-old son Adam down for a nap, and she was looking forward to stretching out on a lawn chair in the backyard and catching up on some reading.

She had not got too far into her book when she heard what she thought was a broken sprinkler hissing. She looked about the yard, glanced toward the screen door that she had left open so she could hear Adam if he should awaken sooner than anticipated. She could see nothing out of the ordinary, and she returned to her reading.

Suddenly, with an icy tremor of fear that shuddered throughout her body, Holly realized that the hissing sound was coming from inside her house. And what was even more unnerving, she could now distinguish the unmistakable buzzing sound of a rattlesnake.

Holly Lenz entered her home to encounter the horror of a four-foot-long coiled rattlesnake in the hallway. The deadly serpent had been halted at the doorway of the bedroom where little Adam was taking his nap. The furry force that held the rattlesnake at bay was their cat, Lucy.

Although the coiled snake kept up its warning rattle and weaved back and forth in a threatening manner, as if prepared to strike at any moment, Lucy refused to back down.

"Clearly Lucy was protecting my little boy," Holly Lenz stated. "She was on her haunches, moving toward the snake very slowly, steadily forcing it back, away from Adam's door."

Ms. Lenz called 911 and carefully moved behind Lucy toward the bedroom. She got there just in time. The toddler was up from his nap and was about to walk out in the hallway. Holly scooped up her son and carried him to safety.

Within a few minutes, the police and an animal control worker arrived at the home. The animal control officer caught the rattlesnake with a loop at the end of a pole, and a sheriff's deputy sliced off its head with a shovel blade.

Holly told reporters that the brave Lucy would thereafter receive nothing but top-grade cat food as a reward for having saved Adam from the reptilian invader.

Oscar the Cat Saves the Life
of a Choking Baby

New mothers who are also cat owners have had to deal with that uneasy old wives' tale about evil felines that suck the breath out of babies as they lie sleeping in their cribs. Kandy Phillips is able to testify that her cat reversed the ancient myth by saving the life of her choking baby.

Kandy, who resides in Modesto, California, was in the kitchen doing dishes one afternoon in the fall of 1990 when her cat Oscar ran into the room and began a loud yowling. Before she could quiet the noisy cat, Oscar jumped up on the kitchen counter.

Irritated by Oscar's blatant disregard of one of the basic "no-no" rules of the house, Kandy brushed him off the counter.

"But even though he knew he would be punished, Oscar jumped right back up," Ms. Phillips said.

This time when she shoved him off the counter, Oscar nipped her on the leg. "He didn't bite me hard, but just enough to let me know that he was really serious about something. Then Oscar started making a lot of noise and began running around in circles."

Totally puzzled by Oscar's bizarre behavior, Kandy Phillips became even more baffled when he ran toward the bedroom where she had just placed her son Anthony for his nap. As far as she knew, her four-month-old baby was sleeping peacefully in his crib.

Out of a mixture of curiosity and annoyance, Kandy followed

Oscar into the bedroom. Once inside, she was astonished when Oscar boldly violated another basic house "no-no" by jumping up on the changing table. Then, before she could even swat him, Oscar had bounded directly into Anthony's crib.

Perhaps dreadful images of all those old tales about cats suffocating infants momentarily flashed before Kandy's mind, but she was soon crying out in a real, not imagined, terror.

Anthony was lying on his side, his face purple, his eyes tightly shut—and he did not appear to be breathing. It was obvious that he had spit up in his sleep and had choked on the vomit.

Trembling in horror, but acting on mother's instinct, she tapped Anthony on his back and attempted mouth-to-mouth resuscitation.

Nothing seemed to help until, in desperation, Kandy held the baby upside down and hit him hard on the back.

"That did it! A stream of vomit left his mouth, and he gasped and brought air back into his lungs. Anthony's crying was music to my ears."

Once her baby was out of danger, Kandy was able to sort out the pieces of the household drama that had nearly become a tragedy. Oscar had saved Anthony's life. If he had not summoned her to the bedroom, her four-month-old son would almost certainly have choked to death.

Something had alerted Oscar to the baby's dangerous situation. Perhaps the child's unusual gagging and choking had disturbed Oscar. Or maybe the cat simply tuned in telepathically to the infant's distress.

Whatever the motivating cause, Oscar was so upset by the baby's situation that he violated all the basic house "no-nos" in order to signal Kandy Phillips that she must check on Anthony at once.

Eleven-Year-Old Boy Survives Frozen Wilderness, Thanks to the Dog That Would Not Leave His Side

For forty-eight hours, eleven-year-old Casey Holliday survived freezing cold, blinding rain, and deadly hailstorms because his faithful mixed-breed St. Bernard, Caleb, refused to leave his side in the frozen wilderness outside of St. Maries, Idaho.

Casey and Caleb had disappeared while on a Sunday afternoon's walk in the fall of 1990. When a freezing rain began to descend upon them, the boy and his dog took shelter in a ravine. By the time the rain had lessened, it was dark—and Casey realized that he didn't know where he was. He was lost. And it was getting colder by the minute.

Casey was getting a little scared, but not much. After all, he had Caleb there with him. And the colder the night became, the closer he snuggled up to the husky, eighty-pound dog.

"It sure was cold out there," Casey said later. "It was thundering and lightning, and both Caleb and I were a little scared. I hung on to him so he wouldn't be scared."

When Casey's aunt, Ginger Holliday, realized that something had gone amiss on the boy's Sunday afternoon outing, she put out a call for help. More than one hundred volunteers and professional rescue workers searched the woods into which Casey and Caleb had vanished.

After forty-eight hours, police authorities were becoming pessimistic. The nighttime temperatures were freezing, and there had been vicious hailstorms that could inflict severe injuries on someone caught unprotected out in the open.

Suddenly Ms. Holliday had a hunch, an impulse that she knew that she must follow. She has since stated that she has no doubt that God guided her to get into her car and begin to drive down a strange road that had been previously neglected. She drove for about five miles when she stopped and shouted her nephew's name.

"Sure enough, he shouted back," Ms. Holliday said. "The two of them were at the foot of a ravine. As amazing as it seems, I had driven right to him."

Rescue helicopters carried Casey, his face blue with cold, to a hospital where he was given fluids intravenously and fed warm broth and juices.

Ginger Holliday stated her conviction that, in addition to providing him with the warmth from his own body heat, Caleb gave Casey "inner strength to hang on and not panic."

Benewah County Undersheriff Alan Riggs observed that Caleb's body heat had protected Casey from hypothermia. In his opinion there was no question that Caleb's presence had made a real difference. "Another night—and who's to say what might have happened?" Riggs noted grimly.

Casey suffered frostbite on both of his feet, and Caleb lost some weight; but the two companions survived the wilderness by sticking together.

Kitten Rescues Mother and Infant Son from Blazing Home

Single mother Corrie Owens of Montreal, Quebec, and her five-month-old son Brandon would have perished in a five-alarm Christmas morning fire if it had not been for the determination of her three-month-old tiger tabby, Jack.

Little Brandon and his mother had returned home to their basement apartment in the early hours of Christmas morning, 1990. "We were dead tired after a family Christmas party," Ms. Owens said, "and we were fast asleep when the fire broke out."

The twenty-two-year-old mother and Concordia University student stated that it was about 6:00 A.M. when Jack hopped on her bed. The kitten began a high-pitched meowing that finally began to pierce Corrie's thick cloud of sleep.

"Only half-awake, I told Jack to be quiet, and I tried to go back to sleep. But thank God, Jack wouldn't shut up. She just kept on with that high-pitched meow of hers."

Then, to her complete horror, Corrie woke up enough to comprehend that their basement apartment was rapidly filling up with smoke.

"I knew that it was a bad fire, and I got really scared. When I got out of bed, I was unable to find any flames, but I was shocked at how thick the smoke was becoming."

Although she was confused, Corrie Owens knew that she dare not panic. She also understood that she and her baby would soon be asphyxiated if they tarried much longer.

She grabbed Brandon and quickly dressed him in some warm clothes. Then she tossed Jack in her travel cage and ran outside with both her babies.

Once outside, she was able to see the nightmarish extent of the blaze. Later she learned that the $300,000 five-alarm fire had started in an adjoining duplex before spreading to her apartment.

Fortunately, Brandon, Jack, and Corrie were able to take refuge in Corrie's mother's home. Jack received a wonderful thank you of a big plate of filet mignon.

"She is my little hero," Corrie Owens said. "If Jack hadn't awakened me with her high-pitched meowing, Brandon and I would have suffocated within minutes."

Family Dog and Two Stray Mutts Save Two-Year-Old from Freezing to Death

It wasn't like little Ernest to wander off. Frail, weighing only eighteen pounds, he was very small for a two-year-old.

But after a two-hour search of the rocky, heavily wooded area around their summer cabin in the rugged hills west of Albuquerque, New Mexico, James and Angeles Mann were forced to conclude that on that June day in 1989, their son had gone for an unauthorized walk with Ivy, the family's spotted white dog.

Mann, a high school mathematics teacher, fought to retain his self-control and not disintegrate into panic. It was already about 8:00 P.M. Although the temperature had been nearly seventy in the daylight hours, he could feel the thermometer dropping fast. Soon it would be in the forties. Overnight it would lower into the thirties.

And little Ernest was wearing only a thin cotton shirt and pants when he walked away from the cabin and into the woods!

The Manns had no choice other than to call Sheriff Ed Craig of Cibola County, who quickly organized a search party of deputies, state police, and volunteers.

James and Angeles felt their hearts sink when the searchers' trained bloodhound was unable to pick up the scent of either Ernest or Ivy.

That was when fear really gripped them. They tried not to consider the possibility that Ernest and Ivy had stumbled upon a mountain lion, a black bear, or a coyote.

Likewise did they strive to eliminate all thoughts that Ernest had been kidnapped and Ivy killed.

Or that Ernest was severely injured and was lying somewhere unconscious and bleeding.

And to add to such agonizing possibilities there was the chilling reality that the night was spreading over the area with a penetrating, numbing cold.

By morning the search party had swelled to more than one hundred officers and volunteers. There were searchers on foot, on horseback, and overhead in an air force helicopter.

It was about 10:00 A.M. when a black dog approached a group of searchers who were walking through a forest clearing. The dog singled out one of the men through a process of selection known only to canine intuition and gently placed his jaws over the man's wrist. The searcher did not have to puzzle over what the dog wanted when it began to tug him in a particular direction.

The searchers followed the dog and their teammate directly to tiny Ernest Mann.

When the black dog seemed certain that the ineffectual humans had actually sighted the boy, it ran over to Ernest, his dog Ivy, and another stray, and snuggled up next to the two-year-old.

Journalist Bennet Bolton quoted Sheriff Craig's fascinating account of the boy's discovery: "Ernest was scared, dirty, confused, but awfully happy to see us. He cried out, 'Doggies, doggies! Warm, warm!' as he hugged them. He was smothered in their hair coats."

The sheriff went on to state that the three dogs had arranged themselves in a tight circle around Ernest, keeping him snug and warm throughout the long, freezing night. "There was no other way the boy—who had wet his pants—could have survived."

Interestingly, as Sheriff Craig carried Ernest to his patrol car, the two stray dogs ran off. It was as if they understood that they were no longer needed once they had accomplished their good deed.

James and Angeles Mann, together with the sheriff and the unselfish, tireless searchers, agreed that Ernest owed his life to the faithful family dog and the two stray mutts that Ivy enlisted to help keep her little master warm until human help arrived.

"Never in all my years in law enforcement—including many searches for people lost in the wilderness—have I seen anything like what those animals did," Sheriff Craig told Bennet Bolton.

Two Mighty Mites Warn Giants To Pick On Someone Their Own Size

Oliver, a tiny, ten-pound Yorkshire terrier, had always subscribed to the old saying: "It isn't the size of the dog in the fight, but the size of the fight in the dog."

It was a lazy afternoon in Buffalo, New York, in the autumn of 1991. Oliver was surveying the neighborhood from his own territory on the Daniel Kennedy lawn when his senses suddenly became alerted to danger approaching the nice elderly lady across the street. Something was wrong with the peaceful picture.

Earlier, Oliver had been watching Lillian Woodside, still energetic at age seventy-nine, raking leaves around her house. The Yorkshire terrier took note that Ms. Lillian's cockapoo, Jackie, was looking after her. Jackie was getting up there, Oliver knew, about thirteen now, but he was still a good watchdog for Ms. Lillian.

Then Oliver focused in on the trouble that he had sensed. An ugly, massive, eighty-pound Akita guard dog had escaped from his backyard next to Ms. Lillian's, and he was heading toward her with blood lust emanating from his brutish brain.

Jackie spotted the giant intruder, and he tried gamely to fend off the Akita. Ms. Lillian poked at the brute with her rake, trying to protect the little cockapoo from the giant's jaws.

Jackie advised a hasty retreat and ran away. But Ms. Lillian didn't have a chance. With a roar of savage fury, the Akita clamped its powerful jaws on Ms. Lillian's arm and began to shake her like a rat. The elderly woman screamed for help as the huge dog began ripping pieces out of her arm—and eating them.

Oliver knew it was up to him to run across the street and save Ms. Lillian.

Daniel Kennedy, Oliver's owner, heard his elderly neighbor's screams, and he also heard the terrible sound of the behemoth's growling and snapping. He headed across the street to help, but he said, "Oliver was a blur racing toward this huge dog on the other side of the street!"

Oliver had come to do battle, and the Akita answered the tiny terrier's challenge. He dropped Ms. Lillian and came for Oliver.

That was what the Yorkshire wanted. He had achieved his goal. Now his owner and other neighbors could pull Ms. Lillian to safety.

After a few snappy exchanges, a couple of bluffs and feints, Oliver decided that discretion was the better part of valor. As he turned to manage a graceful retreat, the Akita snapped two hunks out of his backside.

As if Oliver had planned his moves in advance with a split-second assessment of the situation, he goaded the Akita once more, then scrambled underneath a nearby car that was too low for the mean monster to get at him.

By now, Kennedy had found a big enough stick to drive off the Akita, and he helped his courageous Yorkshire to safety.

Kennedy told reporters that Ms. Lillian's wounds were ghastly. "Nothing was left of her arm but raw meat. That giant dog ripped entire chunks of muscle out of her bicep, tricep, and forearm—and ate them."

Oliver's backside required nine stitches at the vet's.

Ms. Lillian recovered to sing the praises of the mighty mite who had come to save her. "Thank God," she said. "I would have died a horrible death, ripped to shreds and eaten alive, if it hadn't been for that terrific Oliver!"

On October 17, 1990, Teresa Harper had just let her poodle Lacy Jane out into the yard of her Dora, Alabama, home. She had barely had time to close the door when she heard Lacy Jane yelping in pain.

Baffled as to what could possibly be wrong with her poodle, Teresa ran out in the yard to a scene of absolute horror. A massive brown-and-white pit bull had pinned Lacy Jane to the ground and was ripping at her throat with its vicious teeth.

Teresa remembered that she was rooted to the spot, paralyzed with fear. Foam was bubbling from the pit bull's mouth. Lacy Jane's blood was being splattered everywhere.

Teresa said that she had never felt so helpless. Desperately, she tried to pull the giant devil dog off her gentle poodle, but to no avail. She knew that she had to save Lacy Jane from the brute—but how?

That was when she became aware of an angry hiss high above her. It was her cat Sparky.

Sparky had been sitting on top of the porch, about twelve feet up. Perhaps annoyed at first that her nap had been interrupted, Sparky peered over the edge of the roof to perceive the ugly invader grabbing Lacy Jane.

Who did the big creep think he was, barging in on their yard and mangling Lacy Jane? True, the poodle could be a real jerk sometimes, and she was always demanding more than her fair share of attention from Teresa, but after all, Lacy Jane was still her buddy!

Teresa was amazed when Sparky became a four-pound furball from hell and leaped from a height of twelve feet to land directly on the pit bull's head, fiercely sinking all four sets of claws into the monster's flesh.

"Sparky started scratching and clawing and spitting," Teresa Harper told reporter David Wright. "The pit bull brought its head up from Lacy Jane's throat and started jumping."

The astonished pit bull may have begun bucking like a bronco, but Sparky held on like a championship rodeo rider.

The powerful giant managed at last to toss Sparky off its head, but the feisty cat landed deftly on her feet and stood her ground as the pit bull charged.

The brute may have thought he would now make short work of the midget cat and go back to savaging the helpless poodle. Sparky, however, foresaw a very different conclusion to the struggle.

"Sparky reared back on her hind legs like a boxer—and raked her claws right along the pit bull's muzzle," Teresa said proudly. "The pit bull yelped, turned—and ran!"

The veterinarian who stitched Lacy Jane's gaping wounds told Teresa Harper that a vein had been nearly severed in the poodle's neck. If Sparky had not come to the rescue, Lacy Jane would surely have bled to death.

As police searched for the renegade pit bull, Sparky was treated to a can of expensive cat food as a reward. Ms. Harper commented that the feline heroine appeared to feel that it was no more than she deserved.

Algonquin, Sturdy Companion and Protector

In certain of the previous chapters, we've told stories in which pit bulls have definitely figured as vicious villains. In the interest of presenting a balanced picture of the breed, it seems appropriate to present an account in which their owner portrays them as gentle pets and loyal defenders.

Although Tom Muzila, a former Green Beret with a fifth-degree black belt in Shorokan karate, would not seem to require a great deal of protection, he told us that his pit bulls Algonquin and Boadecia had saved his life on more than one occasion.

Muzila recalled the day some years ago when he was climbing a peak in the San Bernardino Mountain range. In those days when he went for a run or a climb, he would hook the pit bulls to a leash around his hips so the three of them could not be separated.

"I had set out on a very steep, one-day climb," Muzila said. "Algonquin was hooked up to the leash around my waist, and we had descended to the tree level in complete darkness. To my distress, I suddenly found that I had lost my sense of direction. As a Green Beret, I had always had an exceptional sense of location and direction, but now I had to admit that I was completely turned around."

To make matters worse, cloudbanks arose and totally obscured the moon. Muzila was acutely aware that sheer cliffs with long drops straight down were all around them. And it was now so dark that he could not even distinguish the trail.

"And it was growing very cold," he said. "I was dressed only in very light clothing since I had expected to be back before dark. I knew that it would drop below freezing that night."

It was at that point that a deeper level of Muzila's consciousness told him to release Algonquin, to allow him to take the lead. Muzila, who has his undergraduate degree in Asian religions, had learned to listen to his inner direction.

"Algonquin led us on what seemed to be a very strange route," Muzila stated. "We went through brush, around trees, over boulders and logs—but I had the sense that we were going down the mountain."

Muzila and his pit bull walked for two hours, following a completely different route from any that Tom had ever before taken.

"Then we followed a dry creek bed for a ways and walked up the bank to emerge directly beside my jeep! Algonquin had led us to safety."

In 1976, when Muzila and Algonquin were jogging on the John Muir Trail, they found themselves out on a ledge with a thousand-foot drop. That in itself was not so bad, but they were suddenly cornered by a very large brown bear.

"Without any concern for his own well-being, Algonquin held off the bear until I could scramble to safety on a higher ledge," Muzila said. "When Algonquin knew that I was out of harm's way, he bounded up the same path to safety, leaving the angry brown bear below us."

Shortly after Muzila left the Special Forces in 1974, he had been hiking the Grand Canyon, intent on viewing the awesome Havasu Falls in the domain of the Havasupai Indians.

"I had been warned about packs of wild dogs that had been raiding various camps and threatening hikers and campers," Muzila said. "I was not particularly worried because I had Algonquin with me, but I appreciated the warning."

As they hiked deep into the canyon, Muzila became aware that they were being stalked. Cautiously glancing over his shoulder from time to time, he was able to count at least six dogs closing in on them.

Algonquin glanced up at his master almost indifferently, as if to say, "Don't trouble yourself, Tom. I'll handle this."

Muzila freed Algonquin from his leash, then climbed up on a large rock to avoid being bitten.

"Algonquin easily fought off all six dogs without sustaining even one bite from their fierce, snapping teeth," Muzila said.

In the period from 1977 to 1980, Muzila, who has also served as technical advisor to numerous martial arts films and has personally trained many movie stars in the various disciplines, spent a great deal of time in a trailer home near Mt. Shasta. At that time, it was a part of his daily exercise routine to undertake a daily run to the top of Bear Mountain.

"On this particular day, I was running as usual, Algonquin leashed to my waist. Suddenly, he started pulling me off the trail, nearly yanking me off balance," Muzila said. "He dragged me almost twenty feet off the trail, barking all the while."

Puzzled by Algonquin's strange behavior, but trusting completely in the pit bull's instincts, Muzila cautiously walked back along the trail.

"There were three huge, coiled rattlesnakes behind some small boulders on the path," he stated. "I would most certainly have jumped over the boulders and landed directly on those deadly rattlers. Somehow, Algonquin had been able to sense their presence far in advance of our approaching them. Once again, my pit bull had saved my life."

When Algonquin died in 1985, he had shared Tom's life for fourteen years. "We had had such a close bond, and I mourned him that night by lighting white candles and saying a prayer for him.

"Later that night," Muzila said, "I was awakened by a familiar scratching at my bedroom door. I knew it was Algonquin. His presence was strong. I drifted back into a light sleep, then I felt him jump on my bed. His loving spirit stayed near me for seven days, then it left to return to the Oneness."

Always At Our Sides To Be Our Guardians and Defenders

Mrs. Eddie Baker of Gallup, New Mexico, stated that she was awakened one night by April, a three-year-old terrier-Chihuahua, and was led into a son's bedroom to find the boy hemorrhaging and choking on blood. Thanks to April's summoning her to the scene, Mrs. Baker was able to save her son's life.

A few months later, Mrs. Baker was led outside by the barking dog and directed to an old refrigerator. When the puzzled woman pried open the door to investigate, she found her seven-year-old son unconscious and near death from asphyxiation.

Benjamin Smith of Lynnwood, Washington, remembered the following story of how their pet bulldog saved the lives of his brother and his uncle:

"Back in the thirties when electricity was still new on the farm, a neighbor constructed a homemade electric fence by using 220-volt direct current, which packed quite a wallop. One day my five-year-old brother and an uncle were walking in an Oregon rain with our pet bulldog, Sarge. My brother, being an inquisitive child, decided to see if the wire of the electric fence would really shock a person in the rain. Again, being a typical boy, he had walked through every mud puddle, thoroughly soaking his feet, thus providing the electricity with excellent grounding.

"Needless to say," Ben continued, "my brother got severely

shocked—to the point where he could not let go. When my uncle saw what had occurred and tried to release him, he found that they were 'frozen' together by the charge of the high-voltage electricity. They would both surely have died within minutes.

"Somehow, Sarge perceived the trouble in which my brother and uncle had placed themselves. With those powerful bulldog jaws, he bit the wire in half. It was as if Sarge knew that he had only a split second to do the deed or he, too, would be frozen by the electrical charge and become as helpless as they were. Although he accomplished the heroic act, he could not escape the effects of the powerful shock. Sarge fell dead the instant after his jaws snapped the wire. My brother and uncle survived only because of Sarge's unselfish act of sacrifice.

"Later, the doctor who examined my brother said that his heart could not have handled very much more of the electrical current.

"I have always wondered," Ben concluded the story, "just how old Sarge could have understood that my brother and uncle were being killed by the wire. And even perceiving that, how did he know that the wire must be cut in order to save their lives?"

King the Superdog Takes Big Bites Out of Crime

Doug McCullough, a cab driver who lives in a high-crime district in Toronto, is the proud owner of a German shepherd named King that seems to have a sixth sense alerting it to any kind of criminal activity. And once King has detected a crime in progress, he rushes to the scene to take a very big bite out of it.

McCullough said that it truly was as if King saw himself as some kind of white knight. "He really sees himself as a protector of women and children," McCullough stated. "King hates crooks of any kind, but if he sees anyone attacking a woman or a child—the bum is dog meat!"

In 1990, King earned a civilian citation from the police for his dramatic rescue of a twenty-year-old woman who was brutally attacked as she walked home in the crime-blighted neighborhood.

Constable Ian Pitcairn told how two thugs jumped the young mother and pulled her into a dark alley. They slammed her up against a garage door, and while one of the creeps held a knife to her throat, the other went through her purse.

It was at that point that King just seemed to materialize out of nowhere. He chased one of the hoodlums over a fence, then returned to lunge repeatedly at the more persistent perpetrator—until he, too, ran away.

Once the muggers were dispersed, King turned his attention to the victim, licking her face and hands and placing his paw on her arm to comfort her.

Doug McCullough said that nothing is capable of frightening King as he patrols the block. The big German shepherd is the self-appointed vigilante of the neighborhood. Since King came on the scene, there have been no successful burglaries on the block.

"If King sees anyone coming around our house who shouldn't be there, he will dive right through the window and grab them," McCullough stated. "The big guy has been hurt on occasion, but that never stops him."

A woman who lived next door to McCullough said that everyone in the neighborhood feels safe with King patrolling the block throughout the night. "We all love him," she said. "We're lucky that he is here to protect us."

Gonzalez had been delayed long enough to be caught red-handed by the police as he was leaving the building.

The investigating officers found Mac unconscious on the floor, but he recovered nicely from the skirmish.

Steve Darensbourg, Glendale police detective, said later that Gonzalez had no idea what had hit him. "All he knew was that some sort of monster was tearing at him with bloodcurdling screams. Mac delayed the burglar for a crucial thirty seconds that allowed us to apprehend the suspect. Considering that the suspect is on probation for another burglary charge, Mac performed a great service."

Paul Scrivano, manager of D'Lights, said that Mac is normally very gentle. He just will not tolerate a thief violating his turf.

"Mac was missing his tail section, and he was in a lot of pain," Scrivano said. "His spirits were down, and he's not talking much."

Gonzalez was charged with felony buglary and cruelty to animals. He pleaded innocent at his arraignment.

Deputy District Attorney Michael Pargament acknowledged that Mac ". . . had delayed the [burglar] long enough so that police were able to catch him as he came out the front door with tools belonging to the store."

In the autumn of 1990, Barbara Platt of Thomaston, Connecticut, discovered that she too had an attack bird.

Ms. Platt found herself in a frightening situation when a drunken man forced his way into her house and demanded to use the telephone. There was something about his crude and rough manner that told her that he wanted more from her than the use of her telephone.

She screamed for help, and Samantha, her twelve-ounce African gray parrot, answered her call.

Before the astonished invader could defend himself, Samantha had dive-bombed him three times, gouging his face with her razor-sharp beak and claws.

At the same time, Gomer, Ms. Platt's fifteen-year-old Chihuahua, decided to join the fray, and she proceeded to sink her tiny teeth into the intruder's leg.

"He started yelling like crazy," Barbara Platt said, "and he ran back into the night, stumbling and screaming in pain. Samantha saved my life!"

Samantha and Gomer were rewarded for their courage with juicy steak dinners.

Baby the Raccoon, Courageous Soldier in the War on Drugs

Far stranger than the dynamic duo of Batman and Robin in the war against drugs and crime is the bizarre partnership of forty-one-year-old Erika Erinwulf (a.k.a. James Lewis Wilson) and his sidekick, Baby the raccoon.

Some years ago, Wilson declared a vendetta against the hardened drug dealers in the Houston neighborhood in which he resides. Dressing as a woman and assuming the personality of "Erika Erinwulf," the determined crimefighter used to carry a .44 Colt handgun in his purse. When his sidearm was stolen, Wilson began carrying Baby, his pet raccoon, with him.

"When I am threatened by thugs, I simply shove Baby in their faces—that always scares them off!"

Although it is unlikely that in even his wildest raccoon dreams Baby ever envisioned himself as a bodyguard for a cross-dressing crimefighter, he appears to have the necessary muscle to send fear into the hearts of hardened drug pushers. Many a tough guy has been rocked back on his heels when Baby was brandished in his face.

Not long ago, when Wilson spoke to journalist Paul Bannister, he claimed that he had already collared twenty drug peddlers for the Houston police.

"I tell them, you may as well move on. The Raccoon Lady is here—and the cops won't be far behind," Wilson said. "Baby and I won't stop until we have driven all of these people out of our neighborhood."

Baby and Erika stake out the abandoned houses where crack dealers hang out. Then they boldly walk in and tell the hoodlums that it is time for them to hit the road.

The police come when he calls, Wilson said, because he does not call as a victim reporting a crime. "I tell them: 'Come and take away this drug dealer I've found.' "

The drug pushers have retaliated by killing Wilson's two pet cats. "They tried to scare me by leaving the skin of one at my door," he remembered angrily.

Wilson has reinforced his apartment so the invaders can no longer penetrate his defenses. "And I've got Baby and an M-1 carbine if they push their luck!"

When Wilson was questioned about a mysterious fire that not long ago destroyed a notorious crack house, he only commented that if the Raccoon Lady and Baby *were* responsible, it would not be very wise to discuss it.

Houston police officer Dana Wagner conceded that the Raccoon Lady and her sidekick had called in the authorities to arrest drug dealers on numerous occasions. "But we don't recommend that the public go into crack houses the way they do. It's dangerous!"

Another Houston cop admitted that the two bizarre crimebusters went into a lot of places where police officers wouldn't go. "What Erika and Baby do is dangerous, but they get arrests."

Sparky Has a Nose for Forbidden Fruit

According to Sparky's boss, Kerry Bryan, a supervisor at Chicago's O'Hare Airport, the talented beagle has a supernose. "He's the smartest little dog I've ever met," Bryan said. "He can zero in on everything from citrus fruit to pork sausages."

Sparky is one of eight beagles that have been trained to sniff out the illegal food stuffs that travelers often attempt to bring into the United States. The detection program is under the aegis of the Department of Agriculture, and Sparky works a tough eight-hour day at the side of his handler, Tommy Miller. Because Sparky is small, cute, and good-natured and does not intimidate people, he is ideal for the job.

Bryan explained that dogs like Sparky are not simply animals trained to bring an additional irritation into the life of a harried traveler on a grueling flight schedule. Sparky and his fellow Department of Agriculture beagles are really protecting our livestock and crops from foreign viruses.

"Just one smuggled orange was responsible for the fruit fly epidemic that hit California in the early 1980s," Bryan said to reporter Lynn Allison. "That one orange ended up costing the taxpayers 100 million dollars!"

Bryan also emphasized that their procedures allowed passengers ample opportunity to declare foodstuffs at customs. "If they don't, Sparky finds the forbidden fruit in their luggage, and we write them a ticket."

Sparky is most often assigned to the "high-risk" flights that arrive from Italy, Poland, Mexico, and India. The beagle with the supernatural nose and his handler, Tommy Miller, patrol the luggage carousels. When Sparky detects the scent of a food product, he sits down and refuses to move. It is that action that serves as Miller's cue to inspect the baggage.

According to Kerry Bryan, Sparky's amazing ability has already recovered the equivalent of the $25,000 it cost to train him.

"He's already found over fifteen hundred pounds of illegal meat in his first twelve months of duty," Bryan told Ms. Allison for the November 21, 1989 issue of Globe. "He's uncovered thousands of illegal fruit and vegetables. One fellow even tried to smuggle in a pair of pigeons from Yugoslavia in a false-bottomed gym bag, but Sparky found them."

Rookie the Narc Says No to Drugs

Police in Tacoma, Washington, have long been proud of their highly trained Labrador retrievers and their keen ability to sniff out illegal drugs.

Then, in 1991, the narcotics officers decided to add another recruit with a sensitive snout to their K-9 corps. Rookie won't bark like the other canine cops, however. He will let out a lusty *oink* when he uncovers a cache of cocaine or marijuana. Rookie, you see, is not a dog. He is a Vietnamese potbellied pig.

Deputy John Jimenez, master trainer for the Tacoma area narcotics and police dog program, rates the pig's intelligence as equal to that of his dogs. "Rookie can already sniff out marijuana," Jimenez said. "When he's located some, he tells us by nosing around for a while, then sitting down."

Jimenez stated that when Rookie is fully trained, he will be able to sniff out hashish, cocaine, heroin, and methamphetamines. The master trainer expects Rookie to emerge as the star of their drug education programs.

The potbellied pig is completely housebroken and shares his abode with six dogs, several cats, and a cow.

Rookie takes a backseat to his canine companions when it comes to jumping up on high places to search for drugs—and admittedly his work pace is considerably slower than that of his buddies in the drug program.

"But Rookie comes on command," Deputy Jimenez said, stressing the porker's positive points. "And he is very good at searching under a car or a truck."

Beatrice Leydecker of Los Angeles is one of a number of paranormally gifted people who can "talk" to animals and assist pets and their owners to develop a more harmonious living relationship. (*Photo credit: The motion picture Unknown Powers, winner of the Film Advisory Board Award of Excellence for 1978; a Don Como film, script by Como, Richard Kroy, and Brad Steiger*)

The new science of "aura photography" seeks to capture on film the very lifeforce of a living entity. Pictures taken through the Kirlian process record the invisible, electromagnetic emanations that appear to reflect moods, emotions, attitudes, and even aspects of physical and mental health.

Especially for this book, we asked Guy Coggins, a leading aura photographer, if he would utilize his sophisticated scientific equipment at his Pro Gen Company in Redwood, California, to attempt to photograph the auras of pets. Here are some of the fascinating results.

This hound gives evidence of a very high degree of mental and spiritual development. Though pictured here in black and white, the aura is predominantly of orange, indicating a strong body; yellow, revealing a careful thought process, and red, suggesting a vigorous lifeforce. Unusual for an animal is the purple arch that surrounds the dog. Purple is the color of high spirituality and/or powerful psychic ability. (*Courtesy of Guy Coggins, Pro Gen Company, Redwood City, CA*)

This horse is bedecked with a glowing aura that reveals lots of red orange and yellow. There seems to be a tinge of green, indicating that the animal is capable of emanating a healing energy. At the very apex of the corona, there is a touch of purple, which represents a high spiritual or psychic faculty. (*Courtesy of Guy Coggins*)

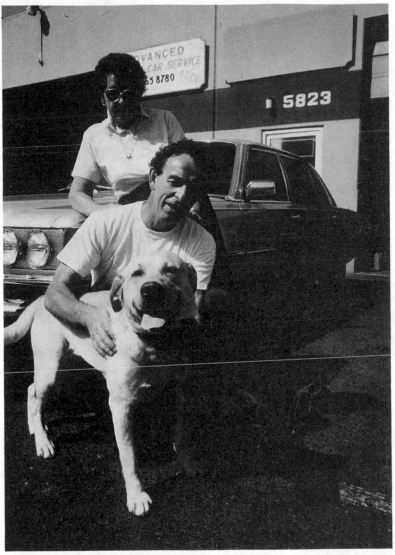

Even though his master, auto mechanic Josef Schwarzl, was over four miles away, Toby, a golden Labrador, knew that he was in danger. Schwarzl owes his life to the fact that Toby alerted his mother and brought her to the garage where he was unconscious from deadly carbon monoxide. (*Photo Credit: Paul Bannister*)

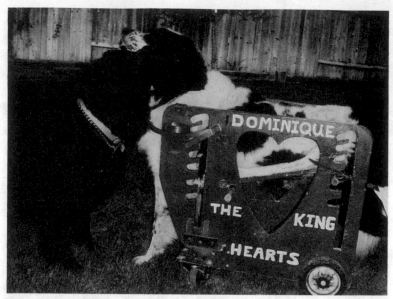

Cathy Mulligan of Phoenix, Arizona, refused to put her beloved 10 year-old 150-pound Newfoundland, Dominique, to sleep when she was told by her veterinarian that Dominique was totally paralyzed in his hind quarters. Cathy, a registered nurse, who specializes in pain and stress management said, "He isn't in any pain, he's just disabled—he can live for a long time yet, but he has to be able to get around." "I couldn't let anything happen to "my boys", they've been here for me through thick and thin when no one else was around," Cathy said passionately.

Shocked that there did not seem to be such a thing as a wheelchair for dogs, Cathy set out to create one! Cathy's love, ingenuity and perseverance, along with the help of friends like Ken Shaw designed and built Dominique his very own doggie-mobile. Cathy said she definitely noticed a change in Dominique's personality when he got his wheels and could get around. He seems happy again—he has his dignity back! Seen here, Dinky gives Dominique encouragement to carry on, as Dominique eagerly gets into his wheelchair. Dominique waits patiently for Cathy to strap him in and put his paralyzed legs into a sling—so they won't drag—then, off he goes. Using his front two legs to pull himself around hasn't slowed him down much. "He even chases cats", Cathy grinned. (*Photo credit: Sherry Steiger*)

Many dogs not only have a super sensitivity for their master, but for other "family" members as well. Here Dinky and Dominique show their affection by touching paws while taking a snooze, almost like humans cuddle. (*Photo credit: Cathy Mulligan*)

Dale W. Olson of Eugene, Oregon, enjoyed a complete and loving relationship with a German shepherd/Norwegian elkhound mix named Ananda. His loyal "Nanda Dog" once saved Olson from drowning when he was whitewater rafting. (*Photo credit: Dale W. Olson*)

Martial artist and film advisor Tom Muzila, with his pit bulls Algonquin and Boadecia. Although a former Green Beret with a fifth-degree Black Belt in Shorokan Karate, Muzila has found himself in situations in which his life was saved by the devotion of his dogs. (*Photo credit: Tom Muzila*)

Muzila works out with Algonquin.

The authors' daughter, Julie Tyree, with her husband, John, and their two "boys," Murphy and Max. Julie has had a close affinity with dogs since her childhood—when her only protector in a haunted house was her beagle, Reb.

Some authorities state that it is possible to learn meaningful clues to your pet's life and development through a numerological analysis of the animal's birthdate and name. These kittens were determined to be Number One cats, that is, pets that will always seek a certain amount of independence. According to techniques provided in this book, it was learned that they will always be obedient cats, but they will want to feel that they can cooperate with their human owner in planning their routine. (*Photo credit: Jon and Patricia Diegel*)

Psychologists have said that the kind of pet that you prefer reveals a great deal about the sort of person you are. For example, cat lovers are most often sensual, captivating people, who have personalities that are fascinating and full of mystery. (*Photo credit: Jon and Patricia Diegel*)

In September of 1984, popular romance novelist Rita Gallagher moved into an old Victorian mansion in the little central Texas town of Navasota. Christening the place "Inspiration House," Rita soon discovered that it housed more than inspiration. She found that the old mansion was filled with noisy and lively ghosts. Her stalwart protector throughout the three-year ordeal was Jupiter, a sturdy German shepherd. In the photograph below, many people claim to see an image of one of the "lady ghosts" directly behind Rita's left shoulder (*Photo credit:* Texas Country)

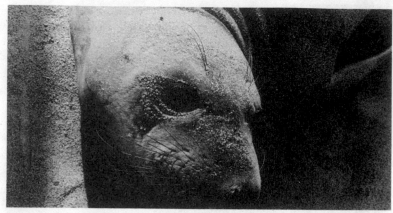

Perhaps animal intelligence has taken a giant leap—or else simply gone unnoticed for so long. There are reports world-wide of animals talking. A sea lion similar to this one was written up as having a vocabulary of some 27 words. Apparently the sea lion just decided to talk one day, as he shocked someone he said "hello" to. (*Photo credit: Sherry Steiger*)

It may have been a dolphin like this one that saved author Sherry Hansen Steiger from a shark attack in 1969, off the coast of South Padre Island in the Gulf of Mexico. After being pulled from the water by an unknown rescuer, Sherry—bloody from head to foot—was taken to the ranger station where a shark's tooth was still embedded in her foot. Dolphins are the *only* known creature of the sea to take on the feared shark. (*Photo credit: Sherry Steiger*)

In 1981, Melissa and her mom, Sherry were kicked out of Sea World for having such a strong bond with the dolphins and whales that the officials feared for the safety of the sea mammals. Pictured here, the authors' daughter, Melissa Hansen revisits Sea World and is so happy she is not ushered out of the park she feeds a dolphin one of his favorite snacks! (*Photo credit: Sarah McWhirter*)

Native American Indians hold a very high regard for all life; but animals have a very special place in the order of things. Some, like the eagle and the toucan and various parrots hold esteemed places. The Feather from these various birds are used in ceremonies. Perhaps they have long known what scientist are just learning: parrots may be as smart as primates! Pictured here is a Medicine Wheel belonging to a medicine woman, Twylah Nitsch, depicting the animal totems of the tribal structure. Twylah is the Repositor of Seneca Wisdom. (*Photo credit: Sherry Steiger*)

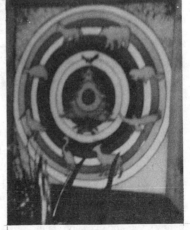

Many people have enjoyed watching monkeys at the zoo. At times their actions seem like a human parody they are putting on to amuse us! Recent scientific research, especially with the chimpanzee, reveals that they are far more intelligent than anyone ever imagined. Chimps have human characteristics such as independence, jealousy, desire, and so on. Film maker Richard Savage developed a unique love bond with Sunday, a Capuchin monkey (pictured below). On one occasion, Sunday warned Savage in time to avoid a dangerous encounter with a 700-pound grizzly bear. (*Photo credit: Paul Bannister*)

Part Three

EERIE ANIMAL TRACKS INTO THE TWILIGHT ZONE

Held Captive by Pets
from Outer Space

On April 2, 1991, a syndicated column entitled "Short Takes" carried an item revealing Brad Steiger's shocking research: "YOUR PET MAY BE A SPACE ALIEN!" Brad was quoted as stating that "one out of five dogs and cats are space pets—descendants of original alien creatures that were 'seeded' on Earth 50,000 years ago. . . ."

The incredible saga of the alien pets began sometime in the spring of 1983 when Brad spoke on the reality of angels to a reporter for the *National Enquirer*. In what he deemed to be a quite moving and inspirational interview, Brad stated his belief that, on occasion, in order to work a miracle—such as saving a drowning infant, rescuing a family from a burning house, and so forth—angels could actually enter the body of a family's pet and temporarily utilize its physical form to accomplish the miraculous deed.

On May 3, 1983, when the interview was published in the *National Enquirer*, Brad was astonished to read the headline: NOTED UFO EXPERT DECLARES: MILLIONS OF PETS ARE REALLY SPACE ALIENS.

In examining the published article, Brad could see that his belief in angels transiently employing the physical bodies of pets had been combined with his well-known Star People research. The article cited the "space pets" as having "charismatic personalities, extremely protective natures, very compelling eyes, and healing powers."

Because of the space pets' great psychic powers, the article continued, "they get along better with humans because they can bond very closely with their masters."

Brad's expression of annoyance provoked the following explanation of editorial rationale:

Since angels are not of this world and exist somewhere "out there" in Heaven—or in space—they may be regarded as "extraterrestrials." Extraterrestrials are commonly referred to as "space aliens." If angels—now "extraterrestrial space aliens"—can temporarily possess pets, then those dogs and cats have thereby been transformed to "alien space pets."

A few months later, in August of 1983, the *National Examiner* managed to discover a Dr. Radj Potel at the "prestigious University of Calcutta," who substantiated Brad's discovery that "one out of five dogs and cats are descended from alien animals."

In 1984, just when Brad thought it was safe to return to the supermarkets, a reporter from *Omni* magazine called to verify his discovery of "alien space pets." When Brad explained the anatomy and evolution of the misquotation to him, the reporter seemed willing to clarify matters. In the pages of *Omni* (February 1985), the angels became "disembodied, superintelligent extraterrestrials" who may enter the bodies of common pets.

As the author of over one hundred books, Brad understands that he is fair game for enterprising journalists. We do not intend any specific criticism of the tabloid newspapers. We believe that when the better ones are at their best, they offer a lively form of reportage and a wealth of human-interest stories. Both of the authors of this book have freely given interviews to various tabloids, and we have appreciated their excerpting and serializing a good number of our books to their diverse and enormous audiences. We only wish at this time to set the record straight on this bizarre misquotation that seems to appear in never-ending cyclical patterns in everything from major metropolitan newspapers to veterinary bulletins and pet lovers' newsletters.

Certainly, among the strange powers of pets are some mighty weird tales that really need no dramatic embellishment or sensationalizing. This section of the book will offer several accounts of some very eerie animal tracks into the Twilight Zone.

Jupiter and the Haunted Texas Mansion

In late September of 1984, popular romance novelist Rita Gallagher moved into an old Victorian mansion in the little central Texas town of Navasota. In Rita's eyes, the house was the perfect writer's retreat that she and her students had dreamed of for so long. She leased the house with an option to buy.

"I was the new kid in town," remembers Rita, author of such novels as *Passion Star* and *Shadows on the Wind*. "No one told me that the house hadn't been lived in for more than ten years—or that it was haunted."

Rita's first night alone in the old mansion explained why the price had been so reasonable. Shortly after 3:00 A.M., there came a rustling in the back hall. Then slow footsteps, with one foot dragging, made their way from the front hall between the bedrooms and descended the main staircase. Though Rita peered up and down the corridor—and even ventured out to the bannister—she saw nothing. There were only the sounds of an invisible presence descending the broad staircase.

And then suddenly she was looking into the sad eyes of a young man with shaving cream on his face—who then promptly disappeared!

"I wouldn't have been afraid if he had stayed and talked to me," Rita said. "The sudden appearance and disappearance of that entity made my first night in the house a terrifying one.

"The next morning, I tested the steps," Rita continued. "The third step down was a creaking one. A board on the top landing had a different sound, and the fourth step above the lower landing creaked more loudly than the others.

"Shortly after 3:00 A.M., these creaking sounds gave the location of the ghost's descent to the main floor. The ghostly walk ended in the kitchen. Until dawn purpled the sky, rattling pots, pans, and dishes echoed faintly through the house. Then the ghost made the trip back upstairs and, with a rustling sound, vanished into the back hall."

Ghost or no ghost, Rita could not afford to lose her investment. And she had a book to write. She decided to work around the ghost and live out the lease.

The next day, she tried to hire a maid and was told in no uncertain tones that there wasn't a maid in town who would *enter* that house, much less work in it.

Rita slept very little in the next two weeks. "Then I realized that since the ghost didn't walk until shortly after 3:00 A.M.—and it never entered my room—I could sleep until that time.

"The Westminster chimes of the clock in the entrance hall tolled the quarter hour, half hour, and hour—until deep night. From 3:00 A.M. until dawn streaked the skies, the chimes were strangely muffled, gurgling as though ringing through water."

It was Rita's habit to leave her bedroom door open and the newel post lamp at the foot of the main staircase burning all night. Light filtered up the open stairwell to the cathedral ceiling on the second floor. Shadows of bannisters on three sides of the stairwell stretched across the wide hall. Though dim, there was always enough light to see anyone—or anything—passing through the corridor.

"I automatically awakened shortly before the rustling sounds began," Rita said, "and I made it my business to stay out of the halls after 3:00 A.M."

With clockwork regularity, after 3:00 A.M. the halls of the mansion were given over to ghosts. After the rustling sounds, the footsteps of what seemed to be an elderly woman wandered the hall, descended the main staircase, and walked back to the kitchen.

"Sometimes, after she reached the kitchen, the rest of the house was silent," Rita said. "Other times, it seemed, her walk evoked further manifestations.

"Now and then I heard an intermittent, murmuring conversation between a man and woman, just low enough that words were indiscernible. Every so often a woman's heartrending sob lasted barely a full second. Occasionally there were knockings and heavy sighs, and once in a while there came the tinkle of glasses, faint piano music, and laughter. Shortly before dawn I was frequently awakened by the sound of something heavy being dragged over the third floor above my room."

In mid-October, Rita went to Beaumont, Texas, for the Golden Triangle Writer's Guild Annual Conference. On the way she planned to visit a friend, a fellow writer living in San Antonio. Upon her arrival, she found her friend crying. Her beloved German shepherd Jupiter was about to be put to death. Her husband had promised to have the deed completed before she returned from the writer's conference.

"I am a dog lover," Rita stated firmly. "Less than a year had passed since my beloved cockapoo, Cleopatra, died of old age. I had never met Jupiter, but I felt a strong compulsion to save him."

Rita learned that her friend, a San Antonio novelist, and her husband had raised Jupiter from a pup. He had registration papers that recorded nine champions in his bloodline, and the first four years of his life had passed uneventfully. Then he had inexplicably changed from a good-natured, obedient pet to an angry, unpredictable behemoth.

Jupiter seemed determined to leave the novelist and her husband, and all attempts to prevent his escapes placed those who would seek to stop him in jeopardy. He had bitten neighbors, friends, meter men, and the postman. Jupiter frequently ended up in the city dog pound for observation.

A week before Rita arrived in San Antonio en route to Beaumont for the writer's conference, Jupiter had chewed his owners' back door frame and had broken free. He had dug up the roses in the neighbors' yard, then run down the street knocking over garbage cans, threatening anyone who came near him.

His record at the county dog pound convinced the authorities that he was a shepherd gone bad. Jupiter was condemned to death.

Rita told Jupiter's owners that she wanted the dog. "I lived two hundred miles from San Antonio. Jupiter would be out of Bexar

County jurisdiction. I would take responsibility for whatever might happen."

After presenting her with a firm warning about the animal's vicious nature, the couple agreed to Rita's terms.

"When the conference in Beaumont was over, I drove back to San Antonio to meet Jupiter," Rita said. "I must admit that the mere size of that magnificent animal was intimidating. He had a great, leonine head and a regal bearing, and he was the size of a half-grown Great Dane. He studied me through intelligent, golden eyes, and I stared at him. It was love at first sight. He walked across the room and placed that giant head in my lap. We were meant for each other."

Without the slightest reluctance, Jupiter left the only home that he had ever known. There were no problems on the long drive from San Antonio to Navasota.

It was three in the afternoon when they arrived at Rita's haunted house. "Jupiter walked into the enormous hall, and I followed him through the loftily ceilinged parlor into the chandeliered dining room, and across the main hall into the library. When we entered the back hall, he paused a moment at the foot of the steep servants' staircase. Staring upward, he sniffed, raised his head abruptly, and whined."

Rita was behind Jupiter all the way as he ascended the servants' staircase to the second floor. His demeanor was calm and certain as he claimed his new domain.

When Jupiter continued up the narrow steps to the third floor, Rita waited below. "Just before reaching the open landing, he stiffened and his ruff came up like a lion's mane. With an earsplitting howl, he backed swiftly downstairs and, staring intently upward, sat down and pressed against me."

Rita saw nothing, but she felt the same presence that she had noted on her first night in the house.

At the immediate foot of the stairs was a small room that Rita— for no reason that she knew then—called the nursery. "Jupiter didn't move. He sat at my feet, alternately cocking his head, staring, and whining."

Deciding to test him further, Rita opened the door to the nursery. "Curious, Jupiter poked his head into the room. Then, turning quickly, he threw himself against me and literally pushed me from the back of the house into the main hall."

Jupiter and Rita walked together down the wide corridor between spacious bedrooms. Side by side they descended the broad, sweeping staircase into the main entrance hall. Stained glass bordered a wavy window that ended barely an inch above the lower landing, and with a sigh, Jupiter settled down there.

"He had found his place," Rita said. "For the rest of our time in that house, he spent his days gazing at the passing scene. That night, and every night thereafter, he slept on a rug beside the bed in my large second-floor room."

Jupiter's first night in the house was an uneasy one, and he moved restlessly on his rug beside Rita's bed. "When the old lady began walking, Jupiter leaped to his feet, nails clicking, and walked across the polished floor to stop just inside the doorway. Cocking his head, he looked out at the dimly lighted hall, first one way, then the other. The footsteps came closer. As they passed my bedroom door, Jupiter's ruff stood straight up. Then, front legs moving like pistons, he slid backwards on his rump over the floor to his rug, where he put his paws over his eyes and gave a low whine."

When the old lady walked on Jupiter's second night in the mansion, he left his rug and went to the foot of Rita's bed. As the ghostly sounds disappeared into the rooms below, he went back to his rug, put his paws over his eyes, and whimpered.

On the third night that the spectral footsteps passed their door, Jupiter raised his head, then went back to sleep. "It was as if he were saying, 'Oh, the hell with it!' "

Two months after Jupiter's arrival, Patricia, one of Rita's students who was going through a divorce, came to live with them in the mansion that had now been christened Inspiration House.

"Jupiter was our protector," Rita said. "He investigated each new manifestation. Then, apparently realizing that there was nothing he could do about it, he made no further effort when it occurred again. He just accepted it—as we learned to do.

"Daylight or darkness, however, he was always alert. Whether alone or together, when my students or I would walk the halls or go upstairs, he appeared beside us. Now and then he would suddenly step in front and gently but firmly push us in the other direction."

Rita was convinced that there was nothing to fear from the ghosts that walked Inspiration House. Except for her encounter with the young man with the shaving cream on his face, none of the entities were ever seen. Although the auditory manifestations were obvious as they moved about the mansion, no psychic-sensitive or paranormal investigator could ever communicate with them.

"For the most part," she observed, "they seemed to be on a never-ending soundtrack, each entity performing intermittently. There was nothing threatening there at all."

But as time went on, Rita discovered that she had been wrong. Something menacing did exist in the old house.

The house had been completely "ghost-free" during the daylight hours; but one late summer afternoon while Rita ran errands, Patricia was seated in the seminar room evaluating manuscripts when a man's heavy footsteps began thudding up the back servants' staircase. Even though Jupiter lay at her feet, Patricia was terrified.

With low, deep, warning growls issuing from his throat, Jupiter chased after the unseen intruder. Summoning her own courage, Patricia followed the German shepherd until the footsteps suddenly ceased in the middle of the main hallway on the second floor. Jupiter whimpered and sat down abruptly. His invisible quarry had vanished completely.

In the days that followed, the heavy footsteps sounded spasmodically through the halls. But Jupiter would only whine and nestle close to Rita's feet.

One afternoon, with Jupiter beside her as usual, Rita was seated with Patricia and the bookkeeper in the large room that they had set up as an office. While Patricia marked manuscripts and the bookkeeper made ledger entries, Rita busily edited the last chapter of her book.

"All at once I was engulfed in a pillar of ice," Rita said. "It was hard to catch my breath, and my heart felt like a large, heavy rock in my chest. I could neither move nor speak. Patricia went on writing; the bookkeeper went on working; and I was terrified!"

"But Jupiter, snarling menacingly, scrambled to his feet. Ruff standing straight up around his neck, he sank his teeth into my heavy slacks and literally pulled me from the chair toward the door. As soon as I left the icy pillar, I could breathe again—but the pain in my chest lasted into the next day. It took even longer to get rid of the chill. It was then that I realized something in the house was far from benign."

Two days later, while Rita was writing upstairs with Jupiter at her feet, the bookkeeper became enveloped in the deadly chill. This time, however, it was Patricia who pulled her free from the icy spell.

"Ministers, priests, and psychic investigators came to Inspiration House, and all confirmed what we already knew. There were multiple hauntings in the old mansion," Rita said. "There was the old woman; the young man; a younger woman; a child; the heavy man whose footsteps sounded intermittently throughout our afternoons—and a threatening entity that seemed determined to snuff out my life and that of my bookkeeper."

Several psychic-sensitives stated that Jupiter was a highly evolved animal that had never turned "bad." On some level of awareness, Jupiter knew that his destiny was intertwined with Rita's and that it was his job to protect her from harm.

"And he did that beautifully," Rita agreed enthusiastically. "During his four years with me, Jupiter protected me from both seen and unseen predators; and throughout all that time, he was a model of propriety. Jupiter the renegade had turned into Jupiter the guardian."

More than a thousand writers and others associated with the publishing world visited Inspiration House during the years that Rita and Jupiter shared their turf with denizens from the spirit world.

"Taking the newcomer's hand as he or she entered, I would introduce Jupiter to each person who visited us," Rita said. "When he saw them welcomed, he went back to his watching place at the landing window near the front door."

It was quite a different story for those "visitors" who had not been officially introduced to Jupiter by Rita.

"Drawn by media publicity, burglars tried to break into Inspiration House. After three attempts, they gave up. Each time they attempted entry, Jupiter's alligator jaws and deep, thunderous barks made their efforts fruitless."

In spite of the rumors about Inspiration House being haunted, students, editors, and agents came there to participate in various writing programs sponsored by Rita Gallagher.

"Some students left after the first night and thereafter came only for daytime tutoring," Rita said. "Others, traveling from greater distances, stayed at a nearby motel. Only after we left that Victorian mansion did we begin to hear stories of what had happened to various guests who had stayed at Inspiration House."

Rita always told guests that bathroom privileges were cut off between 3:00 A.M. and dawn. "Some laughed. Others accepted the edict without question."

Jupiter became not only Rita's guardian and that of her secretary, but the protector of all who came to Inspiration House. "Always, darkness found him, without being summoned, escorting each guest through the upstairs hall to the bathroom. Then, after waiting outside the door, he conducted them back to their beds."

Often, Rita heard Patricia cry herself out of a nightmare in her room across the hall. Her own dreams, too, were strange and frightening. "I would be brought out of a fearful, surrealistic dream by Jupiter's tongue licking my face," Rita said.

During the two and a half years that he and Rita lived in Inspiration House, Jupiter lost a great deal of weight. He slept little, Rita recalled, and now and then seemed to be tormented by something.

Having at last completed her book, Rita realized how much energy it had taken just to live in the haunted mansion. Although the veterinarian said that Jupiter's health was good, Rita knew that he was suffering. Patricia's divorce was finalized; the novel was finished; so they decided to move.

"Our last two weeks in the house were dreadful," Rita said. "Jupiter was hard-pressed to protect both of us, so he clung to my side.

"Old-fashioned push-button light switches were turned rapidly off and on. Water ran intermittently. Toilets were flushed. Doors slammed. In broad daylight, books were lifted from their shelves, hoisted two or three feet in the air, then dropped to the floor.

"Sometimes Patricia's frantic voice called to me," Rita continued the litany of horror. "With Jupiter beside me, I would run upstairs only to discover that she had been in the kitchen or the downstairs bathroom and hadn't called me at all. Other times, it was my voice that Patricia heard calling her."

Two or three times in those last fearful days in Inspiration House, Jupiter was tormented by unseen entities. "At nine or ten at night, with Patricia in her bed reading and me in mine watching television, Jupiter would lie in the hall between our rooms. Suddenly, ruff high around his neck, he would howl, then scramble to the other end of the hall where, trembling, he cowered in the corner.

"When we went to him, petting him and speaking soothing words, his golden eyes were wide, staring beyond us at something we could not see," Rita said. "Then the torture would continue, and he would scramble to the other end of the upper hall."

In late March of 1987, Rita, Patricia, and Jupiter moved to Conroe, Texas. Instead of a haunted Victorian mansion, the new Inspiration House was a modern fifteen-room home with maids' quarters, wide lawns, trees—and no ghosts!

Now that Jupiter was eating and sleeping regularly, he began to gain weight. He was no longer exhausting himself protecting Rita and Patricia.

"During our stay in the new Inspiration House, there was only one ghostly incident," Rita recalled. "Shortly before Thanksgiving, our Inspiration House attorney, a member of our Board of Directors and a dear friend, died suddenly. Along with Patricia's mother, we attended the funeral."

That evening grew cold, rare for southeast Texas. With a roaring fire in the fireplace and with Jupiter lying on the stone hearth, the three women grew nostalgic. "Staring into the flames, we spoke of our deceased friend," Rita said. "We discussed her love of animals in general and of Jupiter in particular. We spoke of her love of roses and good books. We went over the great times that we had had together. We all loved her—and Jupiter loved her too.

"We had often discussed the question of life after death and told each other that, if at all possible, whoever passed on would give some sign to those left behind.

"Suddenly Jupiter jumped up and ran to the sliding glass doors that opened onto the deck," Rita said. "It was early for his nightly walk, but grabbing a sweater, I opened the doors and followed him outside."

It was an established part of Jupiter's nightly routine to bound down the steps to the garden below. This time, however, with wagging tail, he went to the head of the stairs and stopped.

"Bobbing his head, he emitted glad little cries, exactly as he did when meeting a friend," Rita said. "Puzzled, I leaned against the railing and watched. Then I was overwhelmed by the strong aroma of *roses*! I was enveloped in roses. My nostrils were filled with them, and it seemed my skin was caressed with their soft, velvety touch."

With his tail still wagging, Jupiter bounded joyfully toward the stairs again and halted abruptly. Then whining, tail between his legs, he rejoined Rita.

"When we entered the house, I told the others what had occurred," Rita said. "They expressed regret that I hadn't called them.

"We had tea and continued talking about our friend.

"Less than an hour later, Jupiter jumped up, wagged his tail, and scampered about, making joyful, growly noises in his throat. And all the while *the scent of roses* filled the room. When the scent of roses faded, Jupiter stopped his happy scampering as abruptly as he had begun. Then, head down, he resumed his position on the hearth.

"We all knew that our friend had given us a sign!"

In August of 1988, Jupiter became ill. The vet told Rita that her beloved shepherd had cancer. Two months of medication and the opinions of other veterinarians failed to help Jupiter.

"Jupiter was suffering, and his eyes begged me to put him out of his misery," Rita recalled sadly. "On our last night together, he lay on his rug beside my bed while I spoke softly to him. I thanked him for all he had done to make my life happier. I told him that I loved him, and his eyes told me that he loved me, too.

"The next morning, my son came to take Jupiter to the vet where he was to be put to sleep. I couldn't bear to go.

"Before he left, Jupiter said an eloquent goodbye. He leaned against me, rubbed his head on my leg, and licked my hand. Then, abruptly, he went out the door to his death."

Rita remembered how whenever she had a headache or some other malaise, Jupiter refused to leave her side. "He sensed my slightest agitation, and he tried in every way to comfort me. I grew so accustomed to his presence that even now, four years after his death, I sometimes think he is with me. In that shadowy area between sleeping and waking, I hear the jingle of his collar and feel those golden eyes, filled with love, watching my every move.

"I have loved dogs all my life," Rita concluded, "but I never saw—and never expect to see—an animal as intelligent and as loving as my magnificent Jupiter. He knew my every thought, my every mood, my every fear. And always, *always*, he was there, guarding, guiding, and—most of all—loving those in his care."

The Ghostly Foxhounds and the Phantom Huntsman

A Yorkshire farmer named Ames recently related his strange encounter with the Unknown, a tale that once again illustrates the proposition that certain pets and those who love them can be reunited on the Other Side.

Each year the apples on a certain tree in the yard of his farm would wither before they could be harvested. Ames had the tree checked for blight, invested in a much-advertised brand of fertilizer, and took every precaution that the agronomists recommended, but nothing seemed to help.

Almost by accident, the farmer noticed that the blight of the tree coincided with another strange occurrence on his farm. Ever since he had begun to work the farm, he had noticed that once a year, for a period of several days, he would hear the snarling and barking of foxhounds under the apple tree. Ames had no idea whose dogs they were or from whence they had come. He kept only one dog on the farm.

On a number of occasions, Ames had investigated the raucous canine sounds only to return to his work completely baffled. He was never able to see any foxhounds, and he tried desperately to convince himself that he had not heard any, either.

One day while Ames stood talking to his friend, Charles M., the man became distracted from their conversation and asked about the strange barking sounds issuing from the base of the tree.

"I'm glad that you hear it, too," Ames told Charles. "I was beginning to fear that I might be going mad."

"There's no mistake," his friend frowned. "Those are most certainly the sounds of foxhounds. Let's go have a look."

Both men broke into a trot and arrived at the tree in time to glimpse the misty outline of a huntsman in a green and black riding outfit flailing about with his arms as if fighting off a fierce, snarling pack of invisible dogs. The sounds of angry foxhounds were unmistakable, and the gestures of the phantom huntsman were those of a man engaged in a violent struggle.

Ames and Charles were swept by an eerie sensation. It was immediately apparent to them that they had somehow stumbled onto a ghostly reenactment of some scene of horrible carnage that had once taken place beneath the tree. Before either could free himself from the strange, hypnotic hold of the apparition, the scene began slowly to disintegrate.

"What was that?" Ames managed to whisper after the flailing huntsman and the vicious snarls of the foxhounds had faded back into nothingness.

His friend told him that it was simple enough to say *what* they had seen; but to him, the great question was *why* had they seen it?

After some inquiry, Ames was able to learn that a pack of

foxhounds had been kept on the farm in 1880. According to the story, the huntsman, who cared greatly for the dogs, had developed such a rapport with the animals that they reacted in a manner that was almost human. He was a kindly man who never abused his animals and who spent nearly all his waking hours seeing to their comfort. When the gentle huntsman was killed in an accident, the foxhounds kept up a mournful wailing that lasted for nearly two days.

Their new master had no desire to emulate his predecessor. He was a nasty drunkard, abusive toward everybody and everything when he was in his cups. He took a sadistic glee in tormenting the dogs with generous beatings and miserly food rations. He never stooped to pet a dog if he could more easily kick it.

One day, as if by a prearranged signal, the dogs turned on him en masse, cornered him under the apple tree, and tore him to pieces. From that time on, the fruit of that particular tree never ripened.

"It would appear that I have a ghost on my hands," Ames remarked to his friend, Lieutenant Colonel T. A. Lowe.

"Not just a ghost," Lowe reminded him with a wry smile. "But a whole pack of noisy, spectral hounds."

Lowe, who had some previous experience in psychic matters, suggested that Ames employ a human huntsman in an attempt to call the ghostly hounds away from the haunted apple tree.

"Do you really think that would work?" Ames questioned his friend.

"It is certainly worth a try, isn't it?" Lowe shrugged. "But you must make the attempt now while the cycle of the haunting is in full power."

Ames inquired among the other farmers about a huntsman who was known to be kind to his dogs and who maintained an excellent rapport with them. He managed to locate such a master of hounds, and he briefly explained the situation to him as best he could.

"I want to be certain that I have all this straight, sir," Perkins the huntsman said, raising an eyebrow. "You want me to come out to your farm tonight and have a try at calling some ghostly foxhounds with my horn?"

"I'm perfectly serious about this," Ames told the man. "You'll see for yourself tonight."

That night, at the usual hour, Ames and the huntsman were alerted by the baying of foxhounds under the apple tree.

Perkins, the master of hounds, began to laugh. "Oh, sir, you are not bothered by ghosts, but by real dogs. Evidently somebody near here has been a bit careless with his kennel gates, and a pack of hounds has been doing a bit of midnight marauding, so to speak."

Ames maintained his silence as the two men walked out to the yard.

"Just listen to those good and lusty fellows, would you?" Perkins laughed again, the sounds of the hunt making him tremble with excitement in reflex action. "I wonder what the lads have got treed for themselves?"

The huntsman gave a crack of his whip and called to the dogs. The timbre of authority in his voice had the desired effect. The air around the two men was suddenly filled with the padding of the hounds' invisible feet and the baying from their spectral throats.

"Good lord!" Perkins gasped. "I hear the lads all around me, but I can't see a bloomin' hair of a foxhound anywhere!"

"Go on with it, man!" Ames shouted at the huntsman. "Call them out of here!"

With the handicap of some rapidly chattering teeth, the master of hounds fitted the horn's mouthpiece to his lips and blew the "going home" call.

"At once," Ames concluded his account of the phantom foxhounds, "the ghostly noises faded away—and the two of us were alone."

Zeus Came Back To Ease His Owner's Guilt

Although Clarence Johnson of Jacksonville, Florida, was the proud and contented owner of many fine pets, he had long cherished his favorite cat Zeus, a lordly and beautiful seal point Siamese that he had raised from a kitten.

"There is so much satisfaction to be gained from raising a magnificent animal from a tiny ball of fur to a full-grown lord of the household," Johnson stated. "I had personally nursed Zeus through a number of minor health problems, and he had rewarded me with the greatest gift that a pet can bestow upon a human being—loyalty and affection."

Zeus had a peculiar habit of crawling up on Johnson's chest while he was still in bed in the morning and softly kneading the muscles of his stomach and chest. "It was as if he were gently waking me to fix his breakfast; and as kind of an exchange of energy, he was giving me a massage to help me get up and get going."

Zeus was seven years old when one day in June of 1987 he became seriously ill. Johnson immediately took his pet to a well-equipped animal hospital. There he learned for the first time about cystitis, a condition that the veterinarian told him was a fairly common affliction of male cats.

"The doctor told me that surgery would be to no avail," Johnson sadly recalled. "Even the very best medical treatment would prolong Zeus's life only a very little longer.

"In compassionate but frank terms, the vet told me that if I were to put Zeus to sleep at that time, I would spare him a great deal more suffering. If I selfishly decided to hang on to Zeus until the very end, my beloved cat would die slowly and painfully."

Clarence Johnson was spun into a quandary. One always hopes for a miracle cure. Perhaps Zeus's condition might go into remission.

What if Johnson were to consent to Zeus's mercy killing and some new wonder drug were to be announced next week?

On the other hand, the veterinarian seemed so certain that the act of prolonging Zeus's life would prolong his pain.

"I couldn't bear to be the agent responsible for Zeus's suffering," Johnson said. "I returned the next day and told the vet that I had decided that he should end Zeus's agony."

Once the decision was made, Johnson was engulfed by terrible feelings of guilt. "I knew I had done the right thing, but I kept having this image of Zeus somehow knowing that I had condemned him to death. Certainly he was in pain, but would he be able to understand the concept of mercy killing? Would he comprehend *why* I had condoned his death sentence?"

Even greater depression flooded Johnson's psyche when he began to blame himself for having been inattentive to Zeus's condition.

"Perhaps if I had been more observant I would have spotted the signs of the illness early enough to have done something positive about the condition," he said. "Maybe if I had given him better care, Zeus wouldn't have developed the condition in the first place."

Then one night as Johnson lay reading in his bed prior to falling asleep, he was startled to feel something land on the bed beside him.

"I knew at once that it was Zeus," he said. "I clearly heard the familiar sound of his purring; and even though I could at first see nothing, I felt the gentle touch of his paws begin to knead the muscles of my stomach."

Johnson focused on his most pleasant memories of Zeus, and slowly, dimly, but unmistakably, he saw his pet staring lovingly into his eyes.

"I could feel the strong bond of love and affection that still existed between us," Johnson said. "I knew then that Zeus understood what I had done and that he did not blame me in any way for making the decision that had ended his suffering. He seemed to be telling me that he knew that I had done the best that I could for him."

Clarence Johnson continued to gaze affectionately into Zeus's eyes

Mac the Beaked Crusader
Routs Robber

Shortly after midnight on June 13, 1990, twenty-one-year-old Steve Gonzalez broke into D'Lights, a shop that manufactures commercial lighting, in Glendale, California. As he made his way cautiously toward the pitch-dark rear of the building, Gonzalez was unaware of two important things that would soon cause him a lot of trouble:

1) The store had an alarm system that picked up noises and relayed them to a security firm, which called the police.
2) Mac, a fifteen-year-old macaw, stood guard in person.

As he felt his way in the total darkness, Gonzalez approached Mac's perch. That was when the Beaked Crusader decided that the intruder had come far enough.

Out of the pitch blackness came a screeching, scratching, biting fury. Gonzalez screamed in terror, completely unaware of what kind of demon of the darkness had attacked him.

At the same time that the Big Mac attack was launched against Gonzalez, the security system recorded the macaw's bloodcurdling squawks and screams, and the police were called.

After a violent thirty-second struggle and a badly bitten thumb, Gonzalez at last managed to get a fist clamped around his assailant's tail feathers—and he dashed Mac to the floor.

The would-be burglar, however, was so confused by the night stalker that had screeched and scratched at him from the darkness that he stumbled about in a daze, ignoring all the expensive luxury equipment surrounding him. In his bewilderment, he grabbed eleven wrenches and two steering wheels—then decided to get out of the madhouse.

But thanks to Mac, the featherweight champion of D'Lights,

was becoming quite frightened myself wondering just what in blazes was in my hallway that was so ghastly."

Reluctantly, Karen went to investigate, carrying with her the baseball bat that her father insisted she keep handy under her bed.

She broke into nervous laughter when she saw that the only living thing in the hallway was her little black-and-white terrier, Jiggs.

"You old nut case!" I scolded Juniper. "What's wrong with you? Are you playing some kind of game, pretending that you're afraid of your buddy Jiggs?"

Jiggs just stood there, slowly cocking his head from side to side as he studied his companion's bizarre behavior.

"Jiggs almost looked as if he were sad," Karen said. "As if his feelings were hurt that Juniper would behave that way toward him. At that time, I had had Jiggs for six years and Juniper for four—and the two animals had always got along together just fine."

The doorbell rang, and Karen went to answer it. "Don't take it personally, Jiggs," I told him as I walked to the door. "Juniper is just being weird. Maybe he got into some catnip that we don't know about."

Karen remembered that Jiggs gave a forgiving wag of his tail, as if he understood.

She opened her front door to admit her next-door neighbor, Hank Swanson, who carried the limp body of a small black-and-white terrier in his arms.

"I'm so sorry," Swanson told her. "This van came roaring down the street and hit Jiggs. Didn't even stop. I saw it all happen. He died right away, though. Didn't suffer any."

Karen struggled with reality for several moments before she could speak. It couldn't be Jiggs that Swanson was carrying. She had just spoken to him as she walked to answer the door. Juniper had just been hissing at him as if he were seeing a . . . ghost!

She mumbled her thanks to Mr. Swanson for his concern, then took the crumpled body of her faithful pet in her arms and wept softly. It was Jiggs, all right—his collar, his dog tag, his familiar black-and-white rumpled fur.

Juniper was still frozen in a posture of fear, but there was no longer any image of Jiggs in the hallway.

"When I gently laid Jiggs's body down in his dog bed, Juniper suddenly broke free from the rigid trauma that had held him fast, and he dashed behind a dresser, where he remained for the rest of the evening. It took several days before he was able to enter the hallway without first trembling, then running as fast as he could to the kitchen.

"Jiggs had come to bid us goodbye, but he had nearly scared the life out of Juniper in the process," Karen said.

A Hospital Visit from the Other Side

Back in 1953, when Margaret Manthey was sixteen, she was involved in a serious accident in her hometown of Des Moines, Iowa.

"It was a hot day in August," Margaret said. "My dog Beany and I were staying at my friend Rose Ann's house for a few days while my parents were out of town.

"About four o'clock, we got to talking about how good an ice cream soda would taste at the neighborhood drugstore. The more we talked about it, the more tempting the idea of a cherry or chocolate soda became, so we decided to get on our bikes and race each other to the soda fountain at Murphy's Drugstore."

As the two girls got on their bicycles, Margaret's beagle, Beany, jumped to his feet in great excitement. It appeared that he too was up for a race—even though it was definitely a steamy, dog day afternoon in Iowa.

Beany was Margaret's faithful companion in her turbulent teen years. He listened to all of her complaints about boy friends, teachers, and the "terribly unfair" rules and restrictions of her parents. He never contradicted her or pointed out how wrong many of her decisions were. And when she told Beany a secret, she could be certain that his lips were sealed.

Margaret and Rose Ann were pushing their American Flyer bikes to the maximum, panting, puffing, and laughing at the same time. Beany ran beside them, enjoying the exercise, though he would certainly need to have Margaret beg some water from Mr. Murphy before they started the run back home.

None of them saw the 1948 red Ford coupe that roared past the stop sign after making an incomplete stop. Witnesses said later that the driver seemed in an alcoholic daze or some kind of trance as he accelerated directly toward the teenagers and the beagle.

"The next thing I knew," Margaret said, "was that something hard had hit my side, and I was flying through the air. It seemed to take forever before I hit the sidewalk and rolled over on my back. Everything was spinning crazily around me and becoming the color of blood.

"Rose Ann was kneeling beside me, crying, holding my hand. Faces of men and women bobbed up and down behind her, and I heard a lady say that she had called the police. Everything seemed so unreal. I knew that I was saying something, but my voice sounded so faraway that I couldn't hear what I was saying."

Margaret remembered that it felt as if she lay on the sidewalk for hours before an ambulance came to rush her off to Mercy Hospital, but she later found out from Rose Ann that it was only about six minutes.

Margaret's time in the emergency room is equally distorted in her memory. Although it seemed as though she had broken every bone in her body and skinned every square inch of flesh, she heard the doctor pronounce his decision of "a mild concussion," order two nurses to clean up the scratches, and tell an orderly that the young lady was to spend the next couple of nights in the hospital for observation.

Later, when she lay back against the pillows in her hospital bed, Margaret began to cry. "I wasn't such a grownup person that I didn't want my mommy and daddy there with me. And Beany. How I wished that my best friend in all the world was with me to lick my face and be with me in those strange surroundings! Beany had slept on my bed every night since I was ten. I sure wanted him to cuddle up with me and let me tell him about how miserable I felt."

Margaret finally drifted off to sleep, hoping that in the morning her parents would be there—and that in a couple of days she would be back with Beany.

"During the night I awakened because there was something pushed up against my feet," she said. "I sat up as far as my throbbing head would permit. I was startled to see Beany sleeping near my feet on the white hospital sheets. I was so happy to see him, but I was also concerned about what would happen if any of the nurses discovered a dog in the hospital."

Margaret reached out her arms, and Beany snuggled up next to her and licked her face.

"You sweetie," she laughed softly, feeling the warm tears move over her cheeks. "You missed me so much that you found a way to get into the hospital, didn't you?"

After hugging her beloved beagle for a few moments, her concern for Beany's well-being overcame her joy at having her faithful friend near her. "You'd better go home, boy. They mustn't catch you in here. Go on home. Please. Now."

Beany whined and moved even closer to her chest. Margaret winced at the pain of her bruised ribs. She decided that the best course of action would be to ring for a nurse—and to hope she would be understanding about a pet's great love for its mistress!

"The nurse entered my room with a flashlight, and Beany jumped down off the bed and walked to a shadowy corner," Margaret said. "I explained in my best grownup manner that my dog had missed me so and had been so concerned for me that he had somehow managed to get into the hospital. I asked if some nice person might take my dog back home.

"The nurse moved the flashlight beam all around the room. 'There's no dog in this room,' she told me. When I insisted that Beany was in the corner, she walked to the switch and flicked on the lights. Beany was nowhere to be seen."

The nurse smiled and told Margaret that she must have been dreaming. She got her a glass of water and said that she would bring something to make her sleep better.

"I concluded that Beany must have beat it out of there when he heard the nurse coming," Margaret recalled. "I glanced at the large round wall clock and saw that it was nearly 4:30 A.M. I took the pill the nurse gave me, and I thought that maybe by the time that I woke up, Mom and Dad would be there."

When her parents arrived that morning around ten o'clock, the first thing Margaret wanted after all the hugs and kisses had been exchanged was to hear about Beany. "I hope he got home all right. He sneaked into the hospital last night, so I hope he got back home safely."

The look that passed between her parents hurt Margaret more than the concussion.

"Dad explained that they had arrived back home around 3:30 A.M. They had found a trail of blood that had led to the back porch, one of Beany's favorite hiding places. Beany, they told me, had been hit by the car at the same time that I was. In his pain and confusion, he had run back home. Dad and Mom had sat up with Beany, trying their best to comfort him. Beany had died at about 4:00 A.M.

"I will always cherish the memory of his final visit to me in the hospital—a visit that Beany made from beyond the grave," Margaret said.

Rusty's Return

In the November 1991 issue of *Fate* magazine, that marvelous little journal that since 1948 has been chronicling the strange, the unusual, and the unknown, Carolyn Allman of Albuquerque, New Mexico, shared her account of a kitten that returned from the grave to reassure her owner and to assuage her grief.

According to Mrs. Allman, the illuminating incident occurred in 1974. Because she was home alone most of the day, her husband Everett brought a kitten from the pound to be her companion.

It was the "tiniest little orange bundle of fur" that she had ever seen, ". . . orange and white striped with the biggest blue eyes." Carolyn decided to name him Rusty.

She was amazed that such a little thing could be so loving. Rusty became like a baby to her. He would follow Carolyn around the apartment; and whenever she held him, Rusty would reach up to pat her on the chin with one soft little paw.

"It was as if he was reassuring me," she said. "He was so little that his meow was barely audible."

Carolyn was devastated when, only two months later, her new-found, loving companion died quietly in his sleep.

"I had never before felt such grief over losing a pet," she said. She and her husband buried Rusty at the side of their apartment.

The next evening, as she was taking out the trash, Carolyn opened the door to behold a tiny orange tiger kitten with big blue eyes looking up at her. She was stunned, unable to believe what she was seeing.

As she bent closer to get a better look at the kitten that had materialized on her doorstep, she softly called Rusty's name.

The kitten emitted a familiar soft meow, then quickly ran around the corner of the apartment building.

Carolyn went back into the apartment to grab a flashlight, then set out after the kitten, desperately calling, "Kitty, kitty!"

She searched the surrounding area for fifteen minutes before she sadly concluded that the animal had vanished from sight.

When she came to the base of the tree where they had buried Rusty, she saw the impression of one tiny paw print in the soft dirt.

Turning the flashlight beam upward into the tree limbs and discovering no tiny tiger kitten anywhere in its branches, Carolyn Allman was left with her heartfelt conviction: "Rusty had come back to say goodbye and to let me know that he was all right."

Pepe the Pacifier Came Back
from the Grave

Bryce Bond is one of the world's most respected healers and psychic-sensitives. Host of the popular program "Dimensions in Parapsychology," seen by millions throughout the New York metropolitan area, Bond sees himself fulfilling the duel roles of a journalist and a dynamic practitioner of the healing power of love.

"As a healer," Bond states, "I have been involved for a long time with the aspects of cause and effect. There are many created causations for our stresses and diseases. But what about our animal friends? We must bear in mind that they, too, can be affected by stress, tension, fear, and abuse. Remember, if animals can be trained, they can also be programmed to hold on to stressful conditions. Animals may not always be able to express their feelings—but they do have them."

Bond pointed out that in ancient times kings, pharaohs, and high priests all had animals around them for an express purpose. "These leaders all knew that the animals with which they had surrounded themselves would carry the potential burden of sickness or disease for them. If the leader's eyes were bad, often his animal would soon suffer the blindness. In those days, the various leaders knew that their pets would eventually carry the burden of whatever problem troubled them."

Bond said that the same situation exists today; if there is a great deal of love expressed between a person and his or her pet, the animal will begin to carry its owner's illness.

"When you are ill and your cat lies next to you or sits on your lap, you will be able to sense a heavier-than-usual purring. Your cat is somehow aware of your problem, and in some instinctual way he is giving you healing energy. Sometimes cats will draw the illness into themselves."

When we become emotionally involved with a dog or a cat, Bond pointed out, they become as children in our care. We share a great deal of our time and our love and affection with them, and they in their own way return that love unconditionally.

"Your dog would give up his life for you if you were attacked, but could you give up life for your dog?" Bond asks pointedly. "We serve as teachers to our pets, and they serve as teachers to us. There are no limitations when it comes to gaining enlightenment or to learning lessons."

Bond said that during his marriage of twenty-three years he and his wife purchased a French poodle that they named Pepe. The dog was a black male with a zest for life and for exploration. He was small in size, but large in love. Both Bryce and his wife loved Pepe very much, and he became the child that they had never had. They shared with him a happy balance of love, and Pepe returned that energy of tenderness and affection to them.

"Yet my marriage had its problems," Bond stated. "Although it had its joys and happiness, it also had its fights and bickering. Pepe became the pacifier. He appeared to love both of us equally, and he did not like fighting. When we were quarreling, he would come to both of us and give us a little loving, as if to say, 'Stop! Enough!' "

As the years went on, Bond admitted, the fighting between him and his wife increased and the unhappiness manifested. "Sadly, Pepe took on the frustrations, the anger, the dis-ease, and the pain that we were expressing toward each other. He absorbed the emotional disharmony until it turned into cancer. On one level, we can say that Pepe took on the cancer that was meant for my wife or myself. Remember, he loved us both equally, so he allowed our anger to become manifest in his tiny body."

As the cancer became increasingly painful for Pepe, the Bonds sought professional help for him. "We sought the experts in their fields. They all stated the same thing: Pepe was too far gone. Nothing could be done but to put him to sleep."

Bond did not wish to hear such diagnoses. He became angry with such statements. He would heal Pepe himself. After all, wasn't he a healer?

"My ego had intruded," Bond confessed. "Every night when I gave Pepe healing, he would respond very briefly. He, being more intelligent than I at the time, was trying to tell me something, but I had closed off my inner ear. As I fought the reality that my beloved dog was dying, not once did I ever say, 'God, Your will be done!'"

For two months Bond suffered with anger, frustration, apprehension, and stress. He refused to let Pepe go. He refused to release him.

"I did not surrender to God, that His will be done," Bond acknowledged. "I was only thinking about myself. I loved my dog and I wanted to keep him."

Then one night when Bond returned home from work, he prayed over Pepe and practiced the laying on of hands. Suddenly a very loud voice exploded within his consciousness: "Let him go! Let him go!"

Bond knew then what he must do. "I answered back, 'Okay, God, Your will be done,' and in that very moment, Pepe's pain was eased. I had been holding on to his life. I had been intruding on his natural transition. I believe that Pepe had known his situation. He had suffered the pain. At that very moment, he experienced a release. I felt that he was pleased with my decision—at least my mind wanted to believe that."

Bond called to his wife, who was asleep at the time, and he told her of what he had experienced. She agreed that it was best to permit Pepe to make his transition.

"That night, Pepe had his most restful night since his sickness had begun. The next morning, we called the vet. He told us to bring the dog right away.

"When we were ready to leave the house, all the pain, agony, and inner suffering manifested itself," Bond said. "I was shattered. I tried to be brave."

As was their usual custom, Bond told Pepe to get his leash. Pepe got up immediately, as if there were nothing wrong with him. He walked out in the kitchen without any apparent signs of pain or discomfort, and he carried the leash in his mouth to be placed around his neck. Pepe seemed to be completely healed.

Bond was in a state of shock. Perhaps his healing work had at last taken effect. Perhaps Pepe had been healed. His wife was also amazed when she saw how well Pepe appeared.

"We were torn, shattered, not knowing what to do," Bond recalled. "Pepe seemed so well, and we were in the process of taking our beloved dog to the vet's to be put to sleep!

"Then I stated aloud: 'God, Your will be done!'

"Instantly the answer came: 'Let him go!'

"It was then that I realized that Pepe could not stand up or lie down without agony. I now heard that he was whining constantly. He had only been acting brave for our sake. With that realization, I released Pepe of the emotional hold that I had on him."

As Bond and his wife drove their beloved friend to the veterinarian's office, Pepe seemed to know that he was going on a journey into the Great Mystery.

"As we drove to the vet's, we both reflected on the past fourteen years that we had spent with Pepe. He sensed our suffering. Every time I touched him, he licked my hand as if to say, 'Thank you for letting me go home.' We were both brokenhearted."

When they arrived at the veterinarian's, Pepe jumped out of the car as if he were eager to get on with it. Bond's wife stayed outside, for she could not bear to see her beautiful Pepe put to sleep.

Bond could not restrain himself from asking the doctor if he was absolutely certain that nothing could be done for Pepe.

"Nothing!" the vet said firmly. "In fact, you should have done this two months ago. This poor creature has been in so much pain, and he has suffered far too long."

Bond indicated that the doctor should get it over with. The vet very compassionately explained that Pepe would not feel anything but a very gentle drowsiness before he slipped into endless sleep.

"I took Pepe's head in my hands and held him very close to me," Bond said. "I was half-crying, half-telling him that it was all right. I was with him. He licked my fingers. I kissed him on the top of his head and whispered from my heart, 'I love you. Goodbye, my friend.'"

The doctor administered the lethal injection, and Pepe relaxed and fell asleep. There were no twitching muscles. Pepe had peace-fully gone home.

When Bond came through the front door of the office with Pepe's body in a large plastic bag, his wife burst into tears. They placed their dear friend's body in a wooden box in the back seat.

"We drove seven hours to Virginia to my wife's home," Bond said. "We had agreed to bury Pepe there on my wife's family peanut farm. He had loved it there, because he could run free without any restrictions."

When they arrived on the farm, they discovered that the ground was too frozen to dig a grave. It would be necessary for them to wait until the next day when the weather might be warmer. Pepe's body was left in the box in the car.

"My night was restless," Bond said. "I kept thinking that Pepe was still alive and that he was barking for me. My wife experienced the same thing."

The next day, a man came with pick and shovel and dug a grave for Pepe.

Bond could sense the spirit of Pepe running free and joyful all around them. He removed the plastic bag that wrapped him, covered him with his special blanket, and placed some of Pepe's favorite toys with him in the wooden box. Then he closed the lid for the last time, nailed it shut, buried the box, and covered the area with pine branches.

"The loss of anyone or anything connected to you by the bond of love is painful," he observed. "But as long as I have memory, I shall always be connected with Pepe. He was the child I never had—and he was also a teacher to me."

That night the sound of muffled barking became an obsession with Bond. He strained to hear the sound of Pepe's familiar barking.

At last he bolted from the bed, threw on his robe, and raced downstairs. For a few moments he stood in the open doorway, listening.

"Once again I heard the muffled barking," he said. "Barefooted, I ran outside on the frozen ground to the gravesite. I listened again, placed my ear to the mound of dirt . . . and the barking stopped!"

Had he imagined all of this? Was it only his unconscious protesting the loss of his dear friend? It would be the last time that he ever heard the barking sounds.

Several months after Pepe had died, Bond and his wife decided upon a divorce. At the same time, he had decided to end his career in radio broadcasting. Bond knew that he was at a transition point in his life and that he was being given an opportunity to be of greater service to humankind as a healer.

Three years after Pepe's death, Bond was lying in bed ready for sleep. "My physical body was just about to drift into the sleep state when I felt something jump up on the bed and land at my feet. I thought it was part of my dream cycle. But the something began to circle around, then settle on my feet with physical weight and body heat. My eyes were closed, so I kept them closed. I wanted to experience the experience!"

In Bond's consciousness, he *knew* that it was Pepe come to pay a visit, for the dog had always joined him in bed in just such a manner. "Thank you, God!" he rejoiced in his heart.

Pepe then got up and slowly walked the length of Bond's body until he reached Bond's head. Bond was able to feel a smallish body depressing the mattress with actual physical weight as it moved upward.

"Then Pepe brushed against my face about seven times," Bond said. "I kept my eyes tightly shut. I was overjoyed. I wanted this to happen. I feared that if I opened my eyes, this wonderful experience would cease."

Bond reached out in the darkness, his eyes still closed. "I felt his tail with one hand, his cool, wet nose with the other. Next I moved my hand to his stomach, and as I stroked the area, I felt the small hernia that he had—and I felt him breathe.

"His stomach was soft and warm to the touch," Bond said. "I could smell the scent of him without any mistake. It was my Pepe!

"In spite of my joy, I did not open my eyes throughout the entire experience—which lasted for ten minutes. Then, at last, it dissolved. I once again gave thanks to God for the experience."

After the visitation, Bond fell into a deep and very peaceful sleep.

When he awakened the next morning and replayed the events of the previous evening in his mind, he noticed that there were clumps of black hair wedged under each of his fingernails. Poodle hair.

"I trembled with excitement over the additional proof that Pepe had given me to bring peace to my heart and to demonstrate that he was all right," Bond said.

"Later I had the hairs analyzed by a doctor and a forensic chemist. It was, indeed, poodle hair. And as any poodle owner knows, poodles don't shed. Pepe had provided me with physical proof that consciousness survives. Such events are gifts from God!"

Reb Faces Noisy Farmhouse Ghosts in Iowa

Brad Steiger knew from their first meeting that the beagle was a remarkably intelligent dog. He had been named Reb by the college student whom he had followed home from the streets of Chicago. The student's mother, an editor friend of Brad's, had said that regardless of how fate had brought it together with her son, the dog could not reside in their Old Town apartment.

"That dog belongs in the country," had been her assessment of the beagle's needs. "Brad's kids in Iowa need a dog."

Even though the Steigers lived in town rather than out in the country, Brad acceded to his friend's evaluation of both the dog's and his children's needs, and Reb made the trip from the Windy City to the small village in northeastern Iowa where the Steigers resided in the spring of 1970. The personable beagle became an immediate buddy to the kids—Bryan, 12; Steven, 10; Kari, 8; and Julie, 5. By the time the family actually did move to a place in the country—about four years later—Reb was an integral part of the household.

Brad remembers that Reb seemed to possess a preternatural understanding of matters that would normally lie far beyond his avenues of comprehension. For example, Reb was an excellent watchdog with an uncanny ability to distinguish between strangers who were unknown to the family and visitors who were simply unknown to him. Old college friends whom Brad might not have seen for twenty years could stop by unexpectedly and be given a warm beagle welcome and escort to the front door. On the other hand, door-to-door solicitors and other people who truly were strangers would be held at bay until a family member passed approval.

The place in the country was lovely. Majestic pines, sturdy oaks, and walnut trees flanked a solid, two-story farmhouse with an inviting front porch that sat atop a grassy hill. A picturesque creek with a small bridge led to a lane that brought one to the road into the village. Across from the barn and grain storage shed was a rustic cabin said to be one of the oldest pioneer homes in the county.

Although one got a kind of eerie sensation walking past the old cabin nestled under the walnut trees, the haunting was in the farmhouse.

Psychic friends of Brad's had already picked up on the ghostly energy of the place, and a relative of the former owner teased Brad that he and his family should have some interesting nights after they moved into the farmhouse. From what Brad could learn, the restless spirit was that of "Papa," a stubborn Norwegian who had not tolerated any intrusions of technology such as storm windows, electric lights, and running water. Papa had finally yielded to electricity sometime in the late 1940s, and he surprised everyone by actually enjoying radio programs that featured music.

Brad had to order the digging of a well before he moved into the place. He could not imagine that anyone would wish to carry buckets from the spring near the barn to provide the family with drinking water.

Brad and Reb were the first to be welcomed to the home by the unseen presences that dwelt within. The rest of the family was in town on that Sunday morning. Brad was having some tea and toast and reading the newspaper when Reb began growling and pacing back and forth in the kitchen in a peculiar manner.

Brad got up to open the kitchen door to permit Reb access to the outdoors and to relieve whatever tension might be troubling him. He had no sooner settled himself back into his newspaper when his tranquility was shattered by a violent explosion that seemed to emanate from the basement.

Brad feared that the oil-burning furnace had somehow exploded. He could hear clearly the terrible sounds of the concrete walls collapsing on the washer, the clothes dryer, and other appliances in the basement.

When he opened the door to the basement landing, he expected to be met by billowing clouds of thick black smoke. But the instant that he came to investigate, all sounds of the terrible disturbance ceased. The furnace was undamaged and operating perfectly. The basement walls stood firm and unmarked.

Before Brad could even begin to solve that puzzle, he was startled by the sound of yet another explosion that rocked the old farmhouse. This time, the blast seemed to issue from the massive walk-up attic that he was considering converting into a study for his writing.

Brad ran up the stairs to the kitchen and saw that the blast must have rattled loose the kitchen door, which now stood wide open. Then he pounded up three flights of stairs, fighting back fearsome images of the old brick chimney having collapsed and setting the attic on fire.

As he pushed open the attic door, he was once again amazed to find everything as it should be. Nothing had been damaged, and there appeared no sign of any disturbance that would have resulted in the sounds of a violent explosion.

Brad was barely allowed time to catch his breath when another massive explosion reverberated from the basement. Perhaps all that had gone before was some kind of bizarre dress rehearsal for the rocking blast that had now most certainly destroyed half the basement.

Before Brad could run all the way back down to the basement, he heard what sounded like someone tap-dancing behind the door to his son Steven's bedroom. He knew that he was home alone and that no one in his family tap-danced.

Just then he thought of Reb. The sound of tap-dancing could be the clicking of his nails on the polished wood floor.

Brad remembered the open kitchen door. Reb must have let himself in the house, then followed Brad upstairs. Something had lured the beagle into Steven's room, and when the third blast occurred, the door had swung shut to trap him. He was probably jumping at the door in regular thrusts that brought his nails into rhythmic contact with the floorboards—thus sounding to Brad's confused mind like tap-dancing.

Brad hesitated with his hand on the doorknob. Why wasn't Reb barking to be released? The beagle was very expressive and never shy about communicating frustration or irritation.

Brad experienced an even greater sense of apprehension when he distinctly heard Reb barking *outside* the kitchen door. The dog was still outside.

So once again the question persisted: Who or what continued to dance merrily behind the closed door to Steven's room?

Brad twisted the knob and pushed open the door. The room was empty, and the dancing ceased at once. He felt as though unseen eyes were scrutinizing his every move.

Then yet another violent detonation roared up at him from the basement.

At last his concern over the house being destroyed was yielding to his many years of experience as a psychical researcher. He was beginning to sense a game plan behind the explosions. Some unseen pranksters were deliberately sending him running downstairs and upstairs to investigate violent explosions that didn't really exist.

Brad resolved not to the play the game any longer. He would set about creating a new reality.

He walked back to the kitchen, opened the door that *something* had opened and then closed again, and let Reb back into the house. Then Brad purposefully sat down at the table and resumed reading the Sunday newspaper and enjoying his tea and toast.

Although the explosions, the "tap-dancing," and various rappings continued in diverse parts of the house for about another twenty minutes, the disturbances finally ceased when Brad continued to ignore them. Brad had refused to play their game and had created one of his own: "Ignore the ghosties!"

After first pricking up his ears and cocking his head at the noisy disturbances, Reb seemed content to follow his master's lead. He emitted a noisy yawn of indifference, then stretched out at Brad's feet and fell asleep.

Brad chose not to tell the family about his experience since he did not wish to alarm them or to plant any seeds of fear in any of their psyches.

About three nights later, when he was working late at his office in the village, Brad received an urgent telephone call from his older son Bryan.

"Dad, someone is in the house!" Bryan spoke nervously into the receiver. "Reb and I are in my room. Someone is coming up the stairs. I can hear him move one step at a time!"

Brad could hear Reb's vicious barking and his angry growls and snarls. An intuitive flash assured Brad that no physical invader was threatening his son. The nasty, invisible pranksters were having their fun again.

Brad told his son to try to remain calm. "Put on some music. Distract your mind. I'm on my way home right now!"

It had snowed earlier that day, and Brad prayed for no ice to slow him down on the twelve-minute drive to the farmhouse.

When he arrived at the home, he found all the doors locked. Bryan was still barricaded in his room with Reb and a 12-gauge shotgun. Brad offered silent thanks that the boy hadn't blown any holes in himself, Reb, or the walls.

Later, after he had calmed down, Bryan told of how he had been watching television in the music room (Papa's old bedroom) when he heard what he assumed to be the sound of other family members returning home. He listened to the familiar sounds of an automobile approaching, car doors slamming, voices and laughter, and the stomping of feet on the front porch.

Reb had been lying sleeping at Bryan's feet until the noises sounded on the porch. For some reason that Bryan could not understand at that point, Reb had begun to growl.

"Quiet, boy," Bryan told him. "It's probably Mom and the girls."

But Bryan, too, was surprised to hear the activity on the front porch. It was customary for family members to enter through the kitchen door at the back porch.

He was further baffled when he heard the sound of loud knocking at the front door. Everyone in the family had his or her own key, so why would anyone knock at either the front or the kitchen door?

Bryan begrudgingly stirred himself from his television program and went to admit whoever was pounding on the front door. Reb thrust his head between Bryan's legs as he opened the door. Both boy and beagle were astonished to find the front porch empty.

Then, uttering a sigh of frustration, Bryan heard knocking at the kitchen door. He slammed the front door and began to walk to the kitchen—when the pounding was once again at the front door.

By now he knew that someone was playing a joke on him, and he turned on the yard light so that he could identify the prankster's automobile. He was startled when he saw that his car was the only one in the farmyard.

Fists were now thudding on both front and back doors—and there were rappings at several of the windows. Reb was going crazy, growling and baring his teeth.

Bryan next became aware of an eerie babble of voices and short bursts of laughter. And someone—or something—very large was leaning heavily against the kitchen door, attempting to force it open.

That was when Reb and Bryan retreated upstairs to his bedroom and Bryan called Brad. It took only a few seconds of hearing his son's strained, frightened voice and the angry snarls of the beagle in the background to convince Brad that something was very wrong.

After Brad had heard all of his son's account, they walked around the farmhouse and saw that there were no footprints in the new snow. Neither was there any evidence of tire tracks in the lane. No human tricksters had visited him. But there did exist nonphysical intelligences that would initiate spooky games with anyone they could find who would play along with them.

Early the next evening, at a family meeting, Brad gave his four children instructions on how best to deal with any ghostly manifestations of sound or sight that might frighten them. Under no circumstances should they become defiant or angry. The laws of polarity would only force the unseen entities into coming back with bigger and spookier tricks in response to the aggressive energy directed toward them. Basically, the strategy was to remain as indifferent to the disturbances as possible.

Bryan had already experienced the phenomena firsthand, and he was now better prepared to confront them should they zero in on him again. Steven had chosen to intellectualize the occurrences, and he had decided that they were fascinating. Kari, who at that time had very strong mediumistic abilities, seemed very aware of the presences, but was strangely aloof to them. For hypersensitive Julie, however, it was all too intimidating.

For several weeks after the violent episode with Bryan, things were relatively quiet in the old farmhouse. Then whenever Julie was left alone in the farmhouse with Reb, the entities would gang up on her and the beagle.

It started slowly at first. Perhaps there would be only a weird rapping sound, a short burst of laughter, a sigh or a cry. Not enough to frighten her terribly. But enough to get her attention and to make her anxious.

Then the time came when her brothers and sister were all involved in after-school activities or scheduled work hours at the family store that their mother managed. On those afternoons when Julie would get off the school bus and walk down the lane to find a house empty of all human occupants, she would attempt to brave it out with cookies and milk—and faithful Reb at her side.

Then the weird music would come from Papa's old room. Reb would growl and bare his teeth, doing his best to drive the noisy, unseen presences back; but soon strange voices and laughter were swirling around the beagle and his mistress with such intensity that they would flee the house.

On many late afternoons Brad would return home to find Julie and Reb standing at the end of the lane or seeking refuge at a neighbor's home. On some occasions, Julie would say that she had attempted to call his office, but the voices and the music had invaded the telephone line so that she could not get through.

One night, just as Brad entered his office, he heard the telephone ringing. It was Julie, crying that she had been calling the office ever since Brad had left home. A powerful manifestation had begun almost as soon as Brad's car had disappeared down the lane. From the music room there had throbbed the sound of a drum, a babble of voices, high-pitched laugher, some "funny piano music," and the blaring of horns and trumpets.

Bravely, Julie had tried her very best to remain calm and to act indifferent toward the phenomenon; but as the sounds grew louder and louder, her indifference had dissolved into fear. She knew that Brad was heading for the office, so she just dialed the number and let the telephone ring until he answered it.

Not long after this incident, the Steiger family moved from the haunted farmhouse. Years later, when Brad and his daughter Julie were discussing the bizarre events in the old home, she revealed that it was not until she was a senior in high school that she had been able to identify the eerie music that she had heard issuing from Papa's former bedroom when she was a frightened child of eight.

One night she and some girlfriends had been driving around, listening to one of those radio stations that specialize in nostalgic music from the "good old days." All of a sudden, Julie said that she nearly "freaked out." She was hearing some of the same spooky music that she had heard blaring out at her from that terrible room in that awful old haunted house: Glenn Miller's "In the Mood."

As strange as it may seem, it had been music from the 1940s that had so frightened little Julie. To this day, whenever she hears an old recording of Miller, Benny Goodman, or Duke Ellington, she has to suppress a shiver—for it was their music that she heard echoing from some lost dimension in the darkened recesses of Papa's former bedroom.

Although the old man might not have cared for most of the tools of progress, he must have learned to accept the wonder of radio; and, interestingly, he must have come to tolerate the big band sounds of the 1940s.

Julie can only recall with a shudder that she and the faithful beagle Reb never stayed around long enough to learn to jitterbug.

Their Lives Were Redeemed by a Reincarnated Dog

In 1990, it seemed as though things could not get much worse for 28-year-old April Freeling and her brother Jimmy, 33, of Bristol, Pennsylvania. April had lost custody of her daughter after a nasty divorce. Jimmy had clinically died twice and was having difficulty recovering from major brain surgery.

April admits that they were both about to give up on living when Jimmy discovered that Lady, her loving German shepherd, had been reincarnated to give them a sign of hope.

When she was a child of ten, April befriended an abandoned dog that she named Lady. The German shepherd became her insepara-ble companion for seventeen years until its death in 1990.

"Lady knew my soul better than any human," April told *The Examiner* (November 26, 1991). "But eventually she became ill and had to be put to sleep."

A year later, in the fall of 1991, Jimmy, an electrician, was working at an elementary school when he spotted a German shepherd pup outside the window. Soon after the animal had caught his attention, it began pacing and whining in a way that Jimmy found very familiar. Jimmy admitted later that the dog gave him a "funny feeling," but he ignored it—until the pup suddenly crashed through the window and landed before him unhurt.

Although the German shepherd stayed out of his reach, Jimmy knew then that she was Lady. Later, when he was preparing to go home after completing his work, she jumped into the bed of his pickup and refused to leave.

Jimmy knew that he must bring the dog at once to April.

"I quickly recognized all the habits and mannerisms of my child-hood companion," April stated firmly.

In a manner that did not seem to require the ordinary channels of communication, April was convinced that a loving God had sent her the spiritual essence of Lady to give them strength in their time of need.

"We must keep faith in tough times, because God does *not* forget us!" April said.

Then, sadly, Lady told them that Jimmy must take her back to the school where he found her. She had different owners in her present incarnation. They would be missing her.

April wept as her brother drove off with the pup that currently housed the loving soul of her beloved Lady. Although it was painful to part for a second time, April knew that Lady had once again brought joy to their lives. On a deeper level of understanding, April experienced an inner awareness that things would soon get better for Jimmy and herself.

When Jimmy returned to the schoolyard, he pulled up beside a woman and her crying child. "Have you seen a German shepherd puppy around here, mister?" the seven-year-old boy managed to ask through his tears.

"I think I can help you," Jimmy smiled as he opened the door to the pickup to allow the pup to jump free and return to the arms of its new master.

"They were overjoyed to have her back again," Jimmy said. "Of course I didn't dare tell them just how special that dog was to my sister and myself."

Jimmy stated that he had never been a believer in reincarnation or in any aspect of the paranormal. He admitted that Lady's return had changed his mind.

Other things as well have changed in the lives of Jimmy and his sister. April married again and regained custody of her daughter. Jimmy's health improved dramatically.

"We had given up on things," April confessed, "but Lady's visit a year after her death changed everything. Now life is sweet for us."

The Strangest Pet of All

It was in the fall of 1931 that the mysterious talking animal came to live with the James T. Irving family on the Isle of Man.

His twelve-year-old daughter Voirrey saw it first, just seconds before Irving himself caught a glimpse of it. It was as large as a full-grown rat, with a flat snout and a small yellow face.

"Maybe that's what was making that scratching noise in the parlor last night, Daddy," Voirrey suggested.

The strange beast would not long be satisfied with such simple effects as scratching the beams that partitioned the rooms of the Irving home. It began to mimic the calls and cries of barnyard animals and poultry.

Shortly after the beast's mastery of the language of the barnyard, Irving made a remarkable discovery. The creature was extraordinarily intelligent. Irving or any other member of the family had but to call out the name of a barnyard animal or fowl and the mysterious "rat" would respond with the correct imitation.

The night noises began to increase, and the family was beginning to find them less than pleasant. The animal would hide somewhere in the darkened corners of the bedrooms, blowing, spitting, growling—keeping the family awake until all hours of the night.

Once, in an effort to lull herself to sleep, Voirrey began to chant nursery rhymes aloud. She was startled to hear the weird animal begin to repeat the rhymes after she had finished. In an excited voice, she called to her parents to come and to share her astonishing discovery. The creature could now talk.

Mr. and Mrs. Irving stood at the door of their daughter's bedroom and exchanged incredulous stares. The animal's voice, although a full two octaves higher than any human's, was clear and distinct as it sing-songed nursery rhymes.

Their uninvited guest soon put itself on intimate terms with the Irvings. It hailed Mr. Irving as "Jim" and his wife as "Maggie." It carried on long conversations with them, and announced one day that it had decided to make its permanent home with them.

Such a bit of news was received by the Irving family with a marked lack of enthusiasm. The family had been able to get so little sleep that Irving was almost at the point of selling the farm and leaving the place to the creature. At the same time, he realized that it would not be an easy task to sell a farm that was not only quite isolated but now seemed to have acquired a most unique handicap—a maddeningly, perpetually speaking pet.

And their talking rodent was no longer a family secret. On January 10, 1932, the Manchester *Daily Dispatch* and the London *Daily Sketch* ran articles on the mysterious "talking weasel."

"Have I ever heard a weasel speak?" asked the reporter for the *Daily Dispatch.* "I do not know, but I do know that I heard, today, a voice I never imagined could issue from a human throat."

The journalist stated that he found the Irving family to be ". . . sane, honest, and responsible folk not likely to indulge in difficult, long-drawn-out practical jokes to make them the talk of the world."

James Irving kept insisting to visiting journalists that "there are no spooks here! The farm is not haunted. All that has happened is that a strange animal has taken up its abode here."

Since the first night of the animal's arrival, however, the "talking weasel" had given evidence of some obvious poltergeistic features. Strange scratchings and unexplainable sounds were followed by the equally mysterious and unaccountable moving of furniture and the tossing of small objects.

Taking sudden issue with the journalists' label of a "weasel," the creature all at once declared itself to be a mongoose that had ancestral roots near Delhi, India. As if to prove its announced heritage, the animal began to sing Indian folk songs and to place a smattering of Indian words in its conversation.

The animal's claim of being a mongoose was reinforced by the fact that a farmer in Doarlish Cashen had once brought a number of the creatures to kill off the rabbits that had become a threat to his field crops. No one had ever caught more than a glimpse of the animal that had moved in with the Irvings, but those who had seen the strange thing had described it in terms that might well have applied to a small mongoose.

After proclaiming itself to be a mongoose, the animal seemed intent upon pulling its own weight in the Irving household by providing meat for the family table. Over a period of some weeks, over fifty rabbits were left on the kitchen floor by the suddenly thoughtful mongoose.

It is interesting to note, however, that each of the rabbits had been strangled. If a true weasel or mongoose had done the killing, it would surely have used its teeth on the throat of its prey.

James Irving began calling his mysterious guest Jef, a name that seemed to meet with the approval of the self-proclaimed mongoose.

"When I lived in India, I stayed in the house of a tall man who wore a green turban on his head," Jef informed Irving during one dialogue. "I was born on June 7, 1852."

"But," Irving stammered, "that makes you 79 years old!"

The talkative mongoose laughed and began singing a Hindu folk song.

Jef's activities were by no means confined to the Irving cottage. He wandered far afield to stalk rabbits for the family meal, and he took delight in hiding in village garages and in bringing back gossip to share with the Irvings.

The weird entity also had a cruel streak which it most often indulged on the villagers. Once, it terrorized a group of men repairing a road by carrying off their lunches. Several of the workmen swore that they had seen lunch bags being toted off by some invisible force.

Another time, Jef was blamed for striking a garage mechanic with a large iron bolt. Irving later attested that Jef had boasted of the deed.

Harry Price, the famous British psychical researcher and ghost-hunter, sent Captain Macdonald, an associate, to the Isle of Man to investigate the truth of the news stories that he had begun to collect on the "haunt" of Cashen's Gap. It was a rare stranger that made a favorable impression on Jef, and the investigator Captain Macdonald proved to be no exception to the rule.

"Get him out of here!" Jef screamed from his hiding place. "That bloody man is a doubter!"

When Macdonald stood with camera and tried to coax Jef out of his crack to pose for a picture, the mongoose displayed its displeasure by squirting water on the investigator. Later, it hurled a needle at the man, which missed him and struck a teapot.

"He often throws things at us," Irving told the researcher by way of apologetic explanation.

A few moments later, the mongoose was seen sitting on a wall in the farmyard. "Quickly," Macdonald pleaded with Voirrey, handing her his camera, "see if you can approach it and get a picture of the bloody beast."

The girl began walking toward Jef, speaking to the entity in a low, pleasant voice. She lifted the camera to sight the animal through the viewfinder and lens, but it was gone before she could click the shutter.

Although Captain Macdonald had received little more than Jef's curses for his troubles, he had at least heard the voice of the mysterious mongoose and had got a glimpse of its actual physical body. When Harry Price came out to the island to investigate the disturbances at first hand, the temperamental Jef remained silent during the entire duration of his stay.

Although Jef often seemed genuinely concerned about the Irving family's welfare (witness the providing of freshly killed rabbits for meat), the mongoose did not relish any open expression of affection. Once Margaret Irving put her hand into Jef's hole and began to stroke the animal's fur. She instantly withdrew her hand with a sharp cry of pain. Jef had bitten her and had drawn blood. "His teeth gripped my hand like a vise," she complained.

The fact that Margaret had actually touched the creature encouraged Harry Price to suggest that the Irvings attempt to obtain a bit of Jef's fur for laboratory analysis. As if it had read their thoughts, the mongoose awakened the family late one night and promised them that it was going to present them with "something precious."

Directed to a particular bowl on a shelf in the kitchen, the eager Irvings turned on the lights and hurried quickly downstairs to seek out the appointed receptacle. There, in its center, was a tuft of fur.

The next morning Irving mailed the fur off to Harry Price, who in turn relayed it to the London Zoo. Unfortunately, it turned out that the cunning Jef was just playing another of his pranks. The fur was that of a dog, not a mongoose.

Determined to obtain some shred of tangible evidence of the being's physical existence, Price sent the Irvings four plasticine blocks so that Jef might stamp the impressions of his feet in the doughy material. James Irving set the blocks in Jef's hole and coaxed his bizarre house guest to imprint its feet in the plasticine.

The next morning, the family awakened to Jef's lusty cursing: "It was hard as hell," he complained. "But I did it. Go 'n look!"

This time it seemed as though the mongoose had really cooperated with Price's desire to secure a permanent memento of its visitation to the Irving farmhouse. Excitedly, James shipped the casts off to Price and anxiously went back to the farm to await the results of analysis and identification.

"One print might have been made by a dog," Mr. R. I. Peacock of the British Natural History Museum's Zoological Department concluded. "The others are of no mammal known to me unless it is that of an American raccoon. . . . I must add that I do not think these casts represent foot tracks at all. Most certainly none of them were made by a mongoose."

R. S. Lambert, an associate of Harry Price's, suggested that Jef was voice and nothing more. But many witnesses had seen something scampering about the Irving house and barnyard that was decidedly some kind of physical entity.

James Irving once wrote in the journal that he had kept throughout the duration of the phenomena that Jef had identified himself to Margaret in the following way: "I know what I am, but I shan't tell you. I might let you see me, but not to get to know me. I'm a freak. I've hands and feet. If you saw me, you would be petrified, mummified. I am a ghost in the form of a weasel."

Jef continued to live with the Irvings for four years, alternately chatting with them and cursing them. Then, slowly, the mysterious talking mongoose simply seemed to fade into nothingness and became but another of the Isle of Man's many legends.

Parapsychologists have attributed much of the phenomena that swirled around Jef to be poltergeistic in nature. The haunting that attends the poltergeist (German for "throwing" or "pelting" ghost) is most often associated with a young person entering puberty. Voirrey Irving was nearly thirteen at the onset of the phenomena, and she was long past this stage of her physical and emotional development by the time the disturbances ceased four years later. And most of the manifestations did in fact seem to circle around James Irving, thus suggesting to some parapsychologists that a part of Irving's split-off mind may have somehow entered into the animal's mental orbit and provoked this most unusual form of pet. It may be important to note that James Irving had traveled widely before settling on the Isle of Man. He could speak German, Russian, and a smattering of several Indian dialects.

In 1947, a farmer actually did shoot a mongoose near Cashen's Gap. There was a great deal of conjecture on the part of the villagers whether or not this animal might have been a descendant of one of the mongooses turned loose in 1914, but the farmer was quite certain that the creature had not talked to him before he pulled the trigger.

Your Pet's Days Are Numbered

Some people who practice the ancient science of numerology believe that the totality of human experience can be reduced to the digits one through nine. These single numbers are the essence of all combinations of numbers and their significance.

If it is possible that meaningful clues to one's life and development can be gained through numerology, then it would seem likely that one might apply single-digit essence to achieve a greater understanding of one's pet.

Let us say that you know the birthdate of your pet to be March 29, 1988 (You may not know the exact date, but the month and year are adequate for the process herewith described).

$$\text{M A R C H} \quad 2\,9, \quad 1\,9\,8\,8$$
$$3 \qquad\qquad 1\,1 \qquad\qquad 2\,6$$
$$3 \quad + \quad 1\,1 \quad + \qquad 8 = 2\,2 = 4$$

March is the third month (3); the day, 29, totals the sum of 11. The year 1988 totals to 26, which reduces to 8. Three reduces no further. Eleven, being a Master Number, does not reduce. We now add 3 plus 11 plus 8, which totals 22, which subsequently reduces to 4.

The number 4 is the most important number in your pet's life. It is its destiny, which the pet cannot change, but which it does have the ability—perhaps with your help—to direct. From this number you may determine your pet's potential, its hidden aptitudes, talents, and desires. Your pet's life-path number symbolizes its rate of vibration—its "frequency," so to speak—which indicates its specific assignment in its present life.

What does the number 4 mean? Here, according to several

philosophies of numerology, is the specific meaning for each number, together with the key words to the life-path number indicated:

1—Key word *individualization*
The Number 1 pet is one that will always seek a certain amount of independence. It is important to the Number 1 pet to feel in charge, to be able to demonstrate how capable it is of protecting its human's life and possessions. It will be an obedient animal, but it wants to feel that it is cooperating with its human and not be forced to take orders in a subservient role.

2—Key word *adaptability*
A pet with the Number 2 life-path will naturally be a well-trained and obedient animal. Those animals with this number are exceedingly tranquil in nature. As opposed to the Number 1 pet, the Number 2 is totally contented to be dependent upon its human owner. A pet with the Number 2 life-path is the ideal apartment dweller, for it will be satisfied with sharing a small amount of space with its human. Number 2 are real "love rags," and they are sensitive to rhythm and music.

3—Key word *expressive*
An animal on the life-path of the Number 3 is one that will always be outwardly demonstrative in expressing its emotions. It may often seem as though your Number 3 pet is on the very threshold of speaking to you in recognizable human words. The Number 3 animal loves people, and it will resent being excluded from any social gathering that you might have in your home. In your Number 3 pet's mind, it too is the host of the event.

4—Key word *achieve*
The Number 4 pet is one that can be easily trained to perform tasks that other animals might find far beyond their range of expression. Number 4 pets make excellent guide dogs, police dogs, and circus performers. Four is also the number of the Earth Mother, so it stands

to reason that the Number 4 animal will strive always to serve other beings and to reach continually greater heights of achievement.

5—Key word *freedom*

If you are seeking a loyal friend and companion that is not liable to wander off and leave you for extended periods of time, you would be well advised not to acquire a pet that is a Number 5. The Number 5 pet is easily bored with a regular schedule and a static environment. If you do a great deal of traveling and are able to bring a pet with you on your journeys, the Number 5 will be a joyful fellow wanderer. If you are a homebody rather than a Marco Polo, pick another number.

6—Key word *adjustment*

Six is the number of devotional love. Number 6 pets will serve their human owners quietly, happily, and efficiently. Their very physical presence brings with it a healing balance that will adjust the most inharmonious of conditions. Number 6 pets are true homebodies. They seem to live on the love vibration, and they will be both playmate and protector to your children.

7—Key word *wisdom*

Seven is a "cosmic" number, and great benefits will be brought to the owner of a Number 7 pet without one's actively seeking better opportunities. Number 7 animals are "old souls" that are moving upward on the evolutionary soul scale. You will find that you will have a great many telepathic conversations with your Number 7 pet, and you will no doubt come quickly to realize that you have an animal mystic in your care.

8—Key word *accomplish*

Eight is a power number. The pet with an 8 life-path is willing to work and delights in any opportunity to display its physical prowess and strength. As long as they are shown a modicum of love, Number 8 animals make superb laborers. The best of the plowhorses or the steeds that bore their knights into battle or the magnificent creatures that pulled the wagon trains westward were Number 8 animals. With such strenuous tasks vanishing from our culture, you would serve your Number 8 pet best by taking him for long walks or runs in the country or by allowing it to perform some task, however inconsequential, in your household.

9—Key word *universality*

Nine is the number of Oneness. Those pets born under the vibration of 9 will live completely for their human owners. It will seem as though they have absolutely no desires or feelings of their own. Number 9 pets are most compatible with artistic and inspirational people. You will certainly be aware of telepathic exchanges with your Number 9 animal, and you are certain to achieve new insights into the universality of all life forms if you allow yourself to link your psyche with that of your pet's.

11—A Master Number: Key word *revelation*

The Number 11 animal has manifested to assist its human owner to achieve some mystical or humanitarian goal. Animals on this vibration are on a higher plane than most of their fellow creatures. They seek out humans who are visionaries, dreamers, psychic-sensitives, and idealists. The Number 11 pet will become a partner on the spiritual level, working with its human counterpart to reveal something new and uplifting to the world.

22—A Master Number: Key word *manifest*

You can be certain that American Indian Medicine Priests and shamanic practitioners from other societies have Number 11 and Number 22 guides and guardians at their side. Number 22 animals have come to work with the master magicians, the practical idealists who are devoted to working for the masses for their improvement, expansion, and growth. The pet with the 22 life-path has achieved a spiritual evolution only a few rungs below that of its human master. It has manifested for the sole purpose of assisting its human counterpart to achieve a philanthropic goal that will abet the progress of humankind and the protection of the animal kingdom.

Choosing Your Pet's Name by the Numbers

Your pet's name is very important as it is concerned with sound, a direct manifestation of vibration. Since each letter of the alphabet has its distinctive sound, it follows that each letter would also have its own distinctive number. Using the one-to-nine cycle, it is vital to establish the essence of the number.

The following graph shows how to arrive at the number vibration. If it is your custom to address your pet only by a single name, the process works fine. Lately, however, it seems to have become somewhat fashionable or acceptable to bequeath to your pet your own last name. In the illustration below, we are using our black Labrador, Moses Hansen Steiger, as an example. Study the table below to see how we arrived at the vibratory number of Moses' name, then use it to derive the frequency of your own pet's name.

1	2	3	4	5	6	7	8	9
A	B	C	D	E	F	G	H	I
J	K	L	M	N	O	P	Q	R
S	T	U	V	W	X	Y	Z	

MOSES   HANSEN   STEIGER
4 6 1 5 1   8 1 5 1 5 5   1 2 5 9 7 5 9
17   25   38
8   7   11 = 26 = 8

Calculating by his single first name, our Moses is an 8; and interestingly, he remains an 8 when we use his full name. And furthermore, our friend is a power number, a dog that delights in work and in serving us—and in receiving our love and going for long, long walks.

Check out your own animal's birthdate and name and see how you have matched—or, Godforbid, mismatched—yourself with your pet.

Discover Your Pet's True Personality in the Stars

Have you ever wondered where your dog got that weird habit of his that seems so unlike that of any canine companions you might have known? Does your cat seem to be walking in space when it is time for it to retire for the night? Has your horse's quirky behavior often appeared to lie beyond any rational explanation?

Accomplished astrologers have told us that the stars and the planets influence animals in many of the same ways that humans are apparently affected by the workings of the heavens. It has always amused us slightly to hear people asking about the sun signs of one another's pets, but it has become very clear to us that many sincere pet owners believe that they can understand their animal's true personality by knowing its birth sign.

Dr. Donald Wolf, a veterinarian from Wheatland, Wyoming, claims to have studied ten thousand cats and dogs for his book, *What Sign Is Your Pet?* He states that "astrology plays an important part in your pet's life."

It is Dr. Wolf's contention that pet owners will have an easier time understanding their animal's many complex and colorful shadings of character by applying the findings of astrology.

After polling a number of professional astrologers, we have put together our own compilation of wisdom from the stars that just might help you learn about your pet and allow you to have an even better relationship.

ARIES: March 21 to April 19
Aries pets are daring, courageous, and extremely energetic. They have a strong independent streak, but they will respond to your loving discipline. They may become nervous or irritable if you needlessly clutter up your life and theirs by inefficiency and improper planning.

Aries animals value order and routine, so it would be best to establish regular times for exercising, eating, and resting. You may find that living with an Aries pet will encourage you to explore areas of mind where you've never before ventured and to experiment with physical activities that you've never before undertaken.

TAURUS: April 20 to May 20

Taurus pets have a great deal of personal magnetism to accompany their tenacious spirit. Their natures are basically very easygoing, and they may be somewhat easier to train than pets born under some of the other signs. Your Taurus pet will love exploring new terrain with you, and you may find yourself releasing a lot of pent-up emotions and hostilities on your long walks. From time to time, your Taurean animal may seem distant and remote. Just give it some time alone, and its warmth and sensitivity toward you will soon return.

GEMINI: May 21 to June 21

Be prepared to get physical with your Gemini pets, for they love to romp about and expend seemingly endless amounts of energy. Gregarious by nature, they love people as well as their fellow animals. They also appear to crave excitement and a steady round of activities. Gemini pets don't like to be left alone, so if you travel a great deal and are unable to bring your pet along with you, you had better find a family member or friend with whom your animal is compatible and who won't mind pet-sitting for you on occasion.

CANCER: June 22 to July 22

Pets born under the sign of Cancer are extremely loyal, which is a good thing because they are also very forward and direct in their behavior. If you have only recently acquired a Cancer pet, it will soon become obvious to you that there may be some difficulty in establishing who is the master and who is the pet. Cancer animals truly enjoy mothering or fathering their owners and their owners' family. Cancer pets also have great powers of concentration and seem to have an almost boundless realm of perception.

LEO: July 23 to August 22
Leo pets have remarkably strong constitutions and great physical stamina. You will also notice at once their sense of pride and self-esteem. As with the Cancer pet, there may be a period of time in which the title of Ruler of the Household may appear to be in question. Leos are born "leaders of the pack," and you must establish early on in your relationship that you are the boss. Never fear, though. While your Leo pet may acquiesce to your leadership, it will remain completely loyal to your regime—as long as you reign with love and kindness.

VIRGO: August 23 to September 22
If your pet was born under the sign of Virgo, you will find it to be an animal with a natural aptitude for learning. Virgo pets have keen minds that are quickly focused, as well as great powers of observation and a good memory for details. Virgo animals are quite easily trained—but never forget to heap praise on them for their efforts. Their extreme sensitivity allows them to be easily hurt, and the slightest scolding will instantly humiliate them.

LIBRA: September 23 to October 23
Libra pets react quickly and negatively to discord and disharmony. They mostly enjoy an environment of symmetry and beauty. You would do well to play soft, classical music in your home if you wish to keep your Libra pet calm and relaxed. The Libra pet has a very sympathetic nature, and you will probably observe that its moods mirror your own on nearly every emotional occasion. You may also notice that your Libra cat or dog will often attempt to mimic your speech tones.

SCORPIO: October 24 to November 21
If you maintain your own balance and an attitude of "tough love" toward your Scorpio pet, things will be fine. Scorpio animals tend to be quite intense and very often extremely aggressive. Don't expect your Scorpio pet to get along very well with other animals—or with your friends. You can more or less anticipate the Scorpio pet to be a

one-person animal. Once you have established workable boundaries for your relationship, your Scorpio pet will never cease loving you and seeking to do its very best to please you.

SAGITTARIUS: November 22 to December 21

The Sagittarius pet is an exceptionally trustworthy animal with great physical magnetism. You will find that your friends and family will be drawn toward your Sagittarius pet, and you will suspect them of being jealous over your acquisition of such a magnificent animal. You will never cease to enjoy the highly charged, affectionate nature of your Sagittarius pet; and you will come to understand how thoroughly the animal's positive energy can lift your spirits on the gloomiest days.

CAPRICORN: December 22 to January 19

The self-sacrificing nature of the Capricorn pet makes it an exceptional animal to watch over young children. Capricorn pets can exhibit such charming personalities and pleasing manners that at times they may seem nearly as human and attentive as a human nanny. Serious in nature, Capricorn pets can become offended and irritated if they feel that they are not being properly appreciated. Improperly handled, a Capricorn animal can appear sullen and moody. Give your Capricorn pet plenty of love, and it will return the emotion a thousandfold.

AQUARIUS: January 20 to February 18

Your Aquarian pet will be an extremely active one—a perpetual-motion machine. Some owners misinterpret their nonstop quest for activity as evidence of a hyperactive nature. Others complain that their animal is scatterbrained or unable to concentrate when it comes time for learning the rules of domesticated living. Aquarian animals are very sensitive, so you must be careful how you approach them at the very beginning of your relationship. Once the two of you work out a balance between your lifestyles, you will find that the Aquarian pet is a true love bug and exceptionally gentle with children.

PISCES: February 19 to March 20

If you like to play loud music around your house or apartment, rattle the pots and pans when you cook, and enjoy a good shouting match with your spouse to release your tensions, then you would be doing a humane act *not* to bring a Pisces pet into your environment. Pisces animals are ruled by their desire for peace and harmony. They are quiet, loving entities, most comfortable with quiet, loving people. Once you have bonded with them in an equitable manner, they will be loyal to the death, content to live in whatever space you are able to provide for them. Pisces pets seem particularly happy around creative, spiritual, and productive people.

Part Four

PETS WITH UNUSUAL TALENTS AND ABILITIES

Lady the Wonder Horse

Over sixty years ago the feats of an apparently ordinary horse that seemed to be able to read, work complicated problems in mathematics, and communicate with human beings served as a major topic of conversation for millions of Americans. Lady Wonder, a three-year-old mare owned by Mrs. Claudia D. Fonda of Richmond, Virginia, was thoroughly studied in 1928 by Dr. J. B. Rhine of Duke University and Dr. William McDougall, a leading psychologist.

For over a month the two scientists conducted a most amazing series of tests with the seemingly gifted black-and-white horse. Even with Mrs. Fonda removed from the scene and with a screen placed between the horse and the experimenters, Lady was able to pick out numbers in answer to arithmetic problems and to select alphabet blocks to spell out words in response to conversational questions. By nudging forward the proper blocks, Lady was able to carry on a dialogue with anyone who desired to question her.

Later Mrs. Fonda and certain researchers developed a "typewriter" on which the letters of the alphabet and the numbers one to nine and zero were arranged in front of the mare, facing the questioners, not Lady Wonder. The talented horse was able to operate this communications device by lowering her muzzle onto levers that would flip up the letters or numbers to provide the answers to the queries directed to her. Such rapid and unerring facility led Dr. Rhine to conclude that animals were able to read the thoughts of humans via some extrasensory capacity.

In a *New York Times* article of May 28, 1928, the writer noted that it seemed a bit unkind to declare Lady a telepathic horse. "This makes it seem," he pointed out, "that Lady performs her miracles merely by mind reading, whereas the investigations might prove that she understands English and arithmetic on her own account."

It does seem, however, as though Lady's most remarkable attributes lay in her seeming powers of prophecy and clairvoyance. Associated Press reporter Paul Duke was astonished when Lady revealed his name, birthplace, and the correct amount of his salary.

It is a matter of documented record that Lady correctly predicted the names of the winners of various heavyweight boxing championship bouts, the entry of the United States and the Soviet Union into World War II, and President Franklin D. Roosevelt's third term in office. Her only notable miss was when she foresaw Thomas Dewey defeating Harry S. Truman in 1948. Asked to explain her inaccurate prognostication, Lady answered: "Funny, he too sure."

Some investigators considered Lady's most remarkable feat to be her role in helping to determine the fate of missing children. When four-year-old Danny Mason was lost in Quincy, Massachusetts, on a harshly cold day in January of 1951, the police were unable to turn up the slightest clue to his whereabouts. Family friends visited Lady Wonder and asked the sensitive mare for her assistance. Lady spelled out *Pittsfield Water Wheel*, which District Attorney Edmund R. Dewing and his staff of detectives sorted out to mean *Pit Field Wilde Water*. When the authorities dragged the Field-Wilde quarry, they found little Danny's body.

In another tragic instance, two children disappeared near Napierville, Illinois, in the winter of 1952–53. When one of the mothers of the missing children came to ask Lady Wonder for help, the horse went to her "typewriter" and stated that the woman would find her son's body in the river near their home. Authorities had already dragged the river, and the current consensus deemed one of two quarries to be the resting place of the children. Great expense was incurred in order to drain both quarries, but the children's bodies were discovered several months later in the nearby river where Lady Wonder had "seen" them.

In mid-March of 1957, Lady Wonder suffered a heart attack, and on March 19th she died. A group of about thirty mourners joined Mrs. Fonda at the funeral in Michael's Road Pet Cemetery in Henrico County.

Karl Krall's Remarkable Elberfeld Stallions

Controversy over the famous "Talking Horses of Elberfeld" spilled over from the universities and gave all of turn-of-the-century Europe a topic for passionate argument regarding the limits of animal training. Professor Edward Claparede, a noted Swiss psychologist from the University of Geneva, Switzerland, declared the revelation of the "talking horses" to be the most sensational event ". . . which has ever appeared in the field of animal psychology—perhaps, indeed, in the whole realm of psychology."

The controversial animal experiments began with a retired mathematics teacher of Elberfeld, Germany, named Wilhelm Von Osten, who had claimed to teach his Russian stallion, Clever Hans, to perform mathematical computations, tell time, and compose intelligent sentences. Thousands of spectators and scientists came to Clever Hans's stall to observe countless demonstrations of the horse's alleged abilities. While many official commissions and committees left Elberfeld completely convinced by what they had seen, just as many left expressing their disbelief.

Von Osten died in 1909 and bequeathed Hans to his friend Karl Krall, a wealthy jeweler, who had come to accept the mathematician's theories about the high intelligence of animals and the training of horses to think and to compute. Krall decided to provide classmates to keep Clever Hans company. He bought two Arabian stallions named Muhamed and Zarif, a blind pony named Berto, and a Shetland pony christened Hanschen. Krall discovered that Von Osten's training methods, combined with a few innovations of his own, soon produced wonder horses that were able to count, add, subtract, multiply, use decimals, read, spell, and respond to questions in a simplified language that he had developed for them to use.

Generally, the talking horses gave their answers by stamping with their hooves in various codes developed by Krall.

Krall found it most interesting that Muhamed, perhaps the more intelligent of the Arabians, soon began to communicate spontaneously. When Krall would enter the stable, Muhamed would sometimes tattle that the groom had beaten Hanschen or that one of the other animals had misbehaved. Sometimes he would even scold his partner Zarif for being lazy.

Once, when the horses were asked to give the cube root of 5,832, one of them stamped out the correct answer—18—while a committee of university scholars were still figuring out the solution on paper.

Such a controversy developed in France, Germany, and England over the true abilities of the trained horses that a special commission was appointed to investigate the true nature of their intellectual capacities. Professor Edward Claparede, one of the leading European authorities on animal psychology, concluded that the Elberfeld stallions were not fakes and that they read and spelled and extracted cube roots by ". . . rational processes rather than by means of trick signs from their trainer."

Dr. Claparede expressed his opinion that the horses were ". . . able to perform many of the tasks which are required of an intelligent schoolboy of fourteen." The psychologist emphasized that he could find "nothing whatever to the idea that [Karl Krall] signals the horses either consciously or unconsciously."

Maurice Maeterlinck, the famous Belgian poet, playwright, and essayist, was among the scientists and scholars who traveled to Elberfeld to investigate Krall's famous thinking horses. Maeterlinck stated that he had investigated the phenomenal animals with the same scrupulous attention that he would have given to a criminal trial.

Maeterlinck wrote that when he saw the horses, he spoke the first word that came into his mind, *Weidenhof*, the name of his hotel. Muhamed immediately "wrote" *Weidenhov*. At this point Krall entered the stable and admonished Muhamed for making an error in spelling. The horse at once tapped out the *f*.

Maeterlinck was greatly impressed by Krall's obvious love for his pupils and the atmosphere of affection that he had created for the horses. "In a manner of speaking," the Belgian poet wrote, "he has humanized them. There are no longer those sudden movements of panic which reveal the ancestral dread of man."

Maeterlinck observed that Krall spoke to the animals in a tender manner, as a loving father might speak to his children. "We have the strange feeling that they listen to all he says and understand it. If they appear not to grasp an explanation or demonstration, he will begin it all over again, analyze it, paraphrase it ten times in succession, with the patience of a mother."

A Dr. Hamel once gave Muhamed the number 7,890,481 and challenged the stallion to produce its fourth root. Within an astonishing six seconds, Muhamed had tapped out the answer, 53. Dr. Hamel checked with a table and was stunned to find that Muhamed was correct. It required eighteen multiplications, ten subtractions, and three divisions to extract the fourth root of a seven-figure number. Muhamed, a "dumb" animal, had managed those thirty-one calculations in six seconds.

Sadly, the incredible Elberfeld horses vanished as draft animals in the horror and gore of World War I. Hanschen, it is said, was eaten during the terrible famine.

In July 1955, Dr. William MacKenzie of Genoa University, president of the Italian Society of Parapsychology, was asked if he remembered the Elberfeld horses from the early days of the century. "Could I forget!" he answered immediately. The only explanation that Dr. MacKenzie could offer was that the famous talking horses were "mediums," possessed by a reasoning mind superior to their own.

Eighty years after their remarkable feats, researchers still argue the intelligence of the Elberfeld horses. Geoffrey Cowley, writing in the May 23, 1988, issue of *Newsweek*, suggests that there was more to the story of Clever Hans and the training methods of Wilhelm Von Osten. A young psychologist named Oskar Pfungst supposedly made the discovery that although Hans succeeded on nine out of ten problems if the interrogator knew the answers, his score plummeted to just one out of ten if the questioner was ignorant of the correct sum.

"Further studies showed that [Hans] had learned to read minds by monitoring subtle changes in [the interrogators'] posture, breathing, and facial expressions," Cowley writes. "So keen was his sense of these cues that informed questioners couldn't conceal them if they tried. Hans could always tell when it was time to stop tapping or moving his head."

Noting that eighty-years-later disclaimer, Cowley nevertheless admits that "[scientists] are acknowledging that while Clever Hans might not have learned math, the knowledge he displayed was awesome just the same."

Would You Believe Talking Animals?

In a balanced article on animal intelligence, "The Wisdom of Animals," in the May 23, 1988, issue of *Newsweek*, Geoffrey Cowley concludes that "even scientists who don't like to speculate about consciousness are parting with the old notion that animal behavior consists entirely of reflexes. There is too much evidence that animals live by their wits."

The scientific debate over whether or not cats, dogs, horses, and other animals can employ rational thought processes will continue for quite some time. In the meantime, serious pet owners have risen above such mundane academic debates and are claiming that not only can their dog or cat think, it can talk to them. That is, they can actually converse, not just imitate human speech sounds.

The Very Loquacious Mr. Lucky

Mrs. J. T. Davis of Midvale, Utah, claimed that Mr. Lucky, a Boston terrier, commanded a speaking vocabulary of twenty words—an assertion that was authenticated by Dr. William Perkins of the University of Southern California's Speech Clinic. According to Dr. Perkins, Mr. Lucky had some difficulty in pronouncing the letters s and r, but his words were still understandable. The Boston terrier's speaking voice was thin and high, somewhat similar to that of a talking doll's mechanical utterances, but his barks and growls were at the customary low pitch.

Mrs. Davis discovered her pet's incredible ability one day when Mr. Lucky had apparently decided that she had tarried too long chatting with a neighbor. The Boston terrier had given her a look of intense boredom and clearly uttered, "Aw, come on home."

In April of 1953, an Associated Press dispatch revealed that reporters from the Salt Lake City *Deseret News* had come back from an interview with Mr. Lucky convinced that the terrier could really talk. "Mr. Lucky doesn't just make unintelligible gruntings that can be interpreted as words," one of the journalists stated. "He makes recognizable words and sentences."

The group of reporters said that they had heard Mr. Lucky pronounce such bits of conversation as the following:

"I want my Mommy," when he was declaring his affection for Mrs. Davis.

"I want some," when he perceived someone eating or drinking something that he liked.

"I will" or "I won't" in appropriate responses to direct questions.

"Oh dear, oh dear," if he got shut up in the basement.

Popular syndicated columnist Ann Landers once published a letter from a woman who insisted that she heard a neighbor's poodle asking to be let outside. Ms. Landers presented the letter in her usual spirited manner and was at once flooded by correspondence from readers who contended that they, too, had talking pets. Excerpts from some of the letters include such comments as the following:

"We have a thirteen-year-old rat terrier who says, "I want out.""

"Our dog says 'Howdy partner,' 'Vas you dere, Cholly?' and 'Goodnight all.' "

"It all started in our house when Heinz [their dog] sneezed and my husband said 'Gesundheit.' We almost fell over when Heinz repeated after him, 'Gesundheit.' "

"Our schnauzer speaks Italian. He says, 'Mamma Signora.' "

Pepe the Talking Chihuahua

One day in the spring of 1965, Rudy Gallucci was called to service the furnace at the Genova residence in Torrance, California.

"Will your dog nip me?" he asked Mrs. Genova, warily eyeing the small Chihuahua sitting on the porch. Gallucci had been bitten before by dogs that appeared friendly.

Mrs. Genova assured the serviceman that Pepe was of a gentle disposition. Gallucci took his customer at her word, walked down to the basement with the Chihuahua at his heels.

"Well, how are you, Pepe?" he asked, wanting to test the dog's true spirit before he turned his back on him and got to work.

"Hello, how are you?" came the reply in a high-pitched voice.

Gallucci's mouth dropped open; his eyes blinked in astonishment.

"I love you," Pepe added.

"I could feel my hair rise," Gallucci said later to a reporter for the local trade newspaper, *Gas News*. "I was actually looking the dog square in the eyes. I saw his mouth open and heard the voice coming out of it."

The serviceman picked up the dog and laughed.

"I love you," Pepe said again.

Gallucci thought that perhaps an operation of some kind had been performed on the dog, "like people do to crows to get them to talk like parrots."

Mrs. Genova laughingly assured him that Pepe could talk, and she even permitted Gallucci to take the dog back to his office so the other service people could enjoy the Chihuahua's high-pitched pronouncements of love.

When free-lance writer Clare Adele Lambert read of Rudy Gallucci's experience, she called Mrs. Genova and told the woman that she simply had to see and hear Pepe for herself. Mrs. Genova graciously extended an invitation to the journalist to visit them. The account of that remarkable visit appeared in the July 1966 issue of *Fate* magazine.

"Hel-*loo*, hel-*loo*, how are you?" the dog greeted Ms. Lambert and her friend when they called at the Genova residence.

Mrs. Genova explained that she had first heard Pepe say, "I love you-oo" one day when she had been hanging some things out to dry on the line. She called for her husband to come outside and the dog said: "How are you? How are you?"

Pepe had been examined by veterinarians who theorized that the extra length of his palate and a peculiar formation of his larynx, combined with a flexibility and mobility of his throat muscles, might give him the ability to produce the sounds of human speech. Some observers also noted that Mrs. Genova spoke to Pepe with exaggerated mouth and tongue movements.

When Ms. Lambert bent close to watch the dog's throat muscles move, she saw Pepe's tongue curve toward the roof of his mouth, as if he were making a conscious effort to form sounds. Such a tongue movement, she rightly observed, is most unusual. Dogs generally keep their tongues down on their lower jaws when emitting sounds.

In Clare Lambert's opinion, Pepe sang rather than talked—"although it is really a combination of both." When the dog was seen to speak, he seemed to concentrate his entire tiny being on his listener. When left alone, Pepe happily licked his fur and ate his food.

A Communicative Cat in Chicago

In November of 1974, Brad Steiger was in Chicago to appear on a number of radio and television shows to promote a recent book. After a late-night talk show he accompanied some friends to the apartment of a local actress for a small party in his honor.

While others helped with refreshments and other arrangements, Brad sat quietly by himself in the front parlor, very much enjoying a few moments of quiet in an exhausting promotion schedule. His reverie was soon interrupted by the sounds of a child calling for his dinner: "Mama," came the voice. "Hungry. Want food now. Want food now, Mama."

Brad knew that the actress had two sons, but since he had just met the woman, he had no idea how old they might be. Obviously, at least one of the boys was quite young, Brad reasoned, perhaps three or four years old.

The voice was nearer now, just beyond the shadows that led down a long hallway. Brad felt certain that the small boy must be watching him from the darkness, like some neglected waif, perhaps feeling resentment toward the stranger that was robbing him of his mother's attention.

At that moment, the front door of the street-level apartment swung noisily open, and two strapping teenage boys entered. It was quite obviously their home.

Brad introduced himself to the friendly teens, still puzzling mentally over the starving waif in the shadows. Then the voice once again issued its pitiful demands: "Eat now. Eat now!"

"Oh, Yama," laughed the younger of the two boys as he walked to the shadowed area just beyond the hall doorway and scooped up a huge gray cat. "Yama, you are always begging for food."

"It's a cat," Brad chuckled. "I thought it was a child."

By now the actress and the other guests had joined Brad in the front parlor. "He *is* a child," she smiled. "He is my big baby."

"Mama!" the large cat scolded from the cradle of the teenager's arms. "Food now. Eat now!"

Later, as supper was served, the actress explained how Yama had begun to talk as a kitten, continuing his articulate demands for food into his adulthood.

Brad has an acquaintance we'll call Hank—who seems to be truthful in all other regards—who insists that a talking cat once paid his family a visit when he was a small boy.

They were first alerted by a scratching at the door. When their father answered the door, a large black cat asked, "Come in?"

"Dad was always game for any adventure," Hank said, "so he made a sweeping motion with his arm and stepped aside to permit the cat to enter. We kids had our mouths hanging open."

Once admitted into the home, the cat pleaded: "Milk? Milk?"

A large saucer of milk was produced, and the strange visitor proceeded to lap it lustily with a long pink tongue. After the bowl had been finished, the cat allowed Hank and his brother and sister to pet it as it lay and purred contentedly before the kitchen stove. Then, suddenly, it got to its feet and proclaimed: "Go now. Out!"

"We begged Dad to let us keep the cat," Hank said, "but such a decision did not seem to be his to make. The cat insisted in a louder tone: 'Go now! Out!'

"Dad opened the door and permitted the cat to continue on its self-appointed rounds. We never saw the strange animal again."

Tramp the Keyboard Virtuoso and Arli the Literary Pooch

Mrs. C. K. Wilderson of north Denver claims to have a dog that plays the piano. The Denver *Post* described Tramp as an eleven-year-old ham performer that took to the keyboard at the slightest encouragement. Striding to the piano, Tramp was said to sit down and begin banging away with both paws. The dog is also reported to keep time with his tail and to yowl lustily in "song" to the accompaniment of his own piano artistry.

Alan McElwaine of the London *Sunday Times* wrote of a dog named Arli that seemed to have mastered the keyboard of a typewriter, thereby becoming a literary, rather than a musical, pooch. Arli was a six-year-old English setter owned by Mrs. Elizabeth Mann Borgese, daughter of the late Nobel Prize-winning author Thomas Mann.

According to McElwaine, the setter used its nose to punch out words of up to four letters. Arli did not begin to display his talent for writing spontaneously one day. Mrs. Borgese admitted that she laboriously taught her pet to hunt and peck at the keyboard. Arli began with *dog* and *cat*, worked up to *bone*, *go bed*, *bad dog*, and so forth.

Dog-Dog Was a Whiz at Arithmetic

A fifteen-month-old cocker spaniel with the awesome monicker of Ginjo Roughneck Sweettooth Chester (Dog-Dog for short) was able to bark out the answers to arithmetic problems, according to his owner, Earl W. Chester of Sacramento, California. Chester put Dog-Dog through his paces for David Deas of the Sacramento *Bee*, and the journalist conceded that the dog's arithmetic was grade-A.

In Deas's opinion, he was convinced that Dog-Dog's ability was not some kind of act devised by Chester to bamboozle the public. Chester himself contended that there was some kind of psychic phenomenon at work.

"How does Dog-Dog understand what I'm saying to him?" Chester asked rhetorically. "We haven't been able to figure it out. He knows these things already, and it's just a matter of studying it and bringing it out."

It's So Nice To Have a Primate Around the House

Sixty-three-year-old Jan Randall of Sunnyside, Washington, is one of those loving women who is happiest when she is mothering somebody. Jan reared two children of her own, then became a second mother to eleven kids when her sister became bedridden with a heart condition. Mothering thirteen children would be more than enough for most women, but not for Jan Randall, who has also taken in more than two hundred foster children.

Mrs. Randall's only worry about mothering lay in the inevitable fact that all of her children would eventually grow up and leave her. Then, about twelve years ago, she found the perfect solution to satisfy her emotional needs when she became the surrogate mother to Chee-Chee, a Manchurian macaque monkey.

In January of 1992, Jan told reporters that the now fully grown, thirty-seven-pound monkey is like Peter Pan, because at the mental age of a five-year-old human child Chee-Chee will never leave her to strike out into the world on his own.

She first acquired Chee-Chee as a newborn infant when a pregnant Manchurian macaque monkey was about to be sacrificed to the cause of medical research. Jan begged for the yet-unborn baby and was present to take the tiny thing into her hands at the moment of its birth. She fed the monkey from a doll's bottle filled with milk and water and treated her as if she were a human baby.

Although Chee-Chee is given no particular household duties to perform, the Randalls stated that three years ago their "baby" alerted the family to a smoldering fire in the attic just before the house burst into flames.

Gene Randall, Jan's husband, went back into the inferno to carry Chee-Chee to safety, declaring to firemen that he had to rescue the monkey since she had saved their lives by sounding an alarm.

Although Robert Foster also refers to his twelve-year-old Capuchin monkey as his "baby," Hellion is a talented housemaid who has been trained to perform multiple duties for her master, who, as a quadriplegic cancer victim, is confined to a wheelchair.

Because of injuries received in an automobile accident when he was only eighteen years old, Foster, 33, is able to move only his head and his shoulders, and his immediate world has been reduced to his Boston apartment. A chin control that has been fitted to his wheelchair enables him to point at objects that he needs Hellion to fetch for him.

A problem inherent in the chin control mechanism is that if it moves even two inches too far to either side, it immobilizes Foster's head. One of Hellion's most important jobs is to nudge the chin control back into place should it ever freeze her master's head movement.

At mealtimes, Hellion scampers across the kitchen floor, opens the refrigerator door, and removes a large plastic container of prepared food. Nimbly, she carries the container in her tiny hands, returns to the table, and carefully spoon-feeds Foster his meal. Should there be any leftovers, Hellion returns the container to the refrigerator.

Mary Joan Willard, founder of Helping Hands, the organization that trained the intelligent little Capuchin to be such an efficient housemaid, told reporter Marie Terry that Hellion was even able to run a carpet sweeper to clean up the kitty litter mess that Foster's two cats had spread across the floor.

The May 15, 1964, issue of *Life* magazine recounted the fascinating working relationship between Lindsay Schmidt, an Australian sheep rancher, and his only permanent farmhand, Johnnie, a monkey that he had obtained when the animal was only a few weeks old.

While it may be impressive to watch Johnnie open bales and spread hay for the sheep, toss grain for the chickens, and assist

Schmidt in herding the livestock, it must be rather amazing to observe the monkey driving the tractor. Not only can Johnnie expertly maneuver the vehicle around rocks and trees, but he can also start the tractor, shift gears, and apply the brakes.

Schmidt never seems to grow tired of telling the story of how he was given Johnnie, then only a few weeks old, by the owners of a traveling circus in gratitude for his having extinguished a fire in one of their trucks. Man and monkey bonded from the beginning of their relationship, and as Johnnie grew older, he seemed eager to help his "father" with the many tasks of farm life.

Schmidt packs two lunch bags, and when it is time to take a noon break, he and Johnnie each has his meal of sandwiches, fruit, and soda. And when it is time to return to their labors, the fastidious Johnnie collects all scraps and litter and disposes of them properly.

In the book *Amazing Animals*, Vida Adamoli writes that the strangest railroad switchman ever employed by a railway was an African baboon named Jack, who "manned" the switches near Vitenhage, South Africa, for nearly a decade in the mid-1800s.

The animal's position of responsibility came when his owner, James Wide, a signalman at the Vitenhage Tower on the Johannesburg-Pretoria Railway, lost both legs in a railway accident. Stubbornly resisting the prospect of a life dependent upon charity, Wide insisted that Jack could assume his job of operating the switches.

Wide was confident of his pet's competence because Jack was already assisting him with such domestic duties as pumping water from the well, weeding and watering the vegetable garden, and keeping their cottage clean.

In their book, *The Strange World of Animals and Pets*, Vincent and Margaret Gaddis pronounce Jack a true anthropoid genius:

"What really brought Jack fame was his ability to operate properly the sets of levers in the tower. He came to know every one of the various block systems, and as the trains sped by he pushed or pulled the levers that set the signals. In addition, when it was required, he operated the tower controls that opened or closed the switches on a siding. . . . For nine years Wide permitted his simian assistant to operate the levers, and during that time Jack never made an error that caused a mishap!"

Adamoli states that the railway, pleased with the clever baboon's work, officially placed Jack on the payroll. His hard-earned wages amounted to twenty cents a day and half a bottle of beer on Saturdays.

When the remarkable Jack died in 1880, he was buried next to the switchbox that he had operated so professionally for nearly a decade.

Amazing Feats of Endurance

The summer of 1990 provided quite a vacation for the Williamson family of New Zealand. First, Trudi, their eighteen-month-old Rottweiler, had given birth to a batch of puppies, and now they cruised along the scenic New Zealand coast in a forty-five-foot boat, delightedly watching dolphins dancing among the waves.

Tragically, it was quite likely during the family's focused attention on the surfacing and plunging marine mammals that Trudi, exhausted from her recent labors, must have fallen overboard. In all the excitement of attending the boat and observing the dolphins at play, several hours passed before twelve-year-old Aaron noticed that his pet was missing.

Robert Williamson turned the craft around at his son's first outcry. They searched and searched; but when darkness came, they were forced to head for land.

Later that night, Robert heard his son's weeping and listened to his desperate prayers for a miracle to bring Trudi back to him.

The next day, Robert tried to explain the somber facts of life to his hopeful son. There really was no chance that Trudi had survived the sea. They had no choice but to return home with her orphaned puppies.

Two weeks later, however, Aaron received his miracle. A group of fishermen had spotted the Rottweiler on an uninhabitable rocky island. When they found the Williamsons' telephone number on Trudi's dog tags, they summoned the joyously astonished father and son to come claim their pet.

Veterinary surgeon Murray Gibb agreed that Trudi's survival and rescue definitely fell within the category of miracles. The doctor theorized that extra body fat acquired during her pregnancy enabled Trudi to resist the numbing cold of the ocean and helped her to stay afloat during an eight-mile swim to the rocky island.

Once on land, however, the Rottweiler found nothing to eat. She had subsisted without food for two weeks until she was found by the fishermen.

Judy, a ten-month-old terrier, survived an astounding thirty-six days trapped underground in a rabbit hole.

It had begun as an ordinary afternoon walk around the family farm for eleven-year-old Evan Davies on that summer's day in 1990. Judy was dashing ahead in the field near the Davies home in Powys, Wales. Spotting a rabbit, the feisty terrier pursued the bunny to its "front door"—as she so often did—but this time she went right on inside Mr. Rabbit's home.

Evan was left standing there openmouthed with shock. Judy had often chased the rabbits to their holes, then bounded away to find new game when the long-eared creatures disappeared into their warrens. Judy had never before taken her pursuit to the rabbits' private domain.

Evan called and called for his pet to return, then ran off sobbing to enlist the help of his mother and sister. That night, after work, Evan's father joined the search for the missing dog.

Although the eleven-year-old boy maintained his faithful vigil for his beloved terrier for several days, his parents tried to console him with promises of obtaining another Judy.

Blinking back his tears, Evan stoutly insisted that there could never be another Judy—and he knew that somehow she was still alive.

until he fell into a deep sleep. "I did not awaken until the next morning, when I opened my eyes to embrace a new day with a total feeling of peace and love toward the wisdom of the universe."

Love Between People and Their Pets That Survives the Grave

Do you believe that your pet will join you in the afterlife?

In a fascinating poll conducted by the *National Enquirer* in 1991, nearly half (49 percent) of the pet owners queried believed that their pet will join them in Heaven. Interestingly, in a five-city poll—Los Angeles, New York, Dallas, Philadelphia, and Washington, D.C.—more men (56 percent) than women (46 percent) expected to spend eternity with their pets.

A Washington speechwriter stated that he did not believe that God would separate a man and his dog.

A Dallas dental assistant believed that pets would accompany their owners to Heaven, because otherwise "they would miss us."

If 49 percent of the pet owners surveyed believe that their pet possesses a soul and will accompany them to Heaven, then we might assume that at least that same percentage of animal lovers might well believe in the spirit of their deceased pet returning to make contact with them or to bid them farewell.

Karen Browne of San Diego told of her strange experience on October 14, 1987, when she heard the unmistakable yowling of her big tabby, Juniper. "I was astonished to see the old guy standing at my bedroom door, looking at something out in the hallway that was obviously terrifying him. His mouth was wide open, hissing and spitting. His ears were drawn back close to his head. Naturally, I

A month later, Malcolm Davies asked his son if he would reconsider the offer of a new puppy. "There's no way that Judy will ever come back to you now, Evan," he said. "You must face the sad truth of the matter."

Evan knew his father meant well, but he asked everyone to wait a little longer. "Judy might show up," he said, more as a plea.

Incredibly, it was only a week later that John Gordon, one of the Davies's neighbors, was awakened at midnight by the sound of a dog barking. Somehow Gordon knew that it was Evan's missing terrier.

About half a mile from his home, Gordon found a skinny, half-starved dog attempting to claw its way out of a rabbit hole. He dug the terrier free with his bare hands, then gave her some food and water. He permitted her only a few moments to rest, then he put her in his car and drove her home to the Davies's farm.

Malcolm and his wife awakened their son with the joyful news that Judy had returned from her thirty-six-day sojourn in the kingdom of the rabbits. Evan jumped from his bed, laughing and sobbing in uncontrollable delight.

Later, an examining veterinarian found that except for a minor eye infection, Judy was surprisingly none the worse for wear after her five-week ordeal. He theorized that the stubborn terrier managed to survive on her own body fat, perhaps a slaughtered rabbit, plant roots, and insects. She must also have found some underground water.

Evans set about fattening up his remarkable pet so that Judy would become so plump she wouldn't be able to squeeze down any more rabbit holes.

Yowser, a five-year-old Brittany spaniel, was left a mangled mess by the massive dump truck that ran over him, but his master's love and his own spaniel spirit managed to pull him through the terrible ordeal.

Donald E. Ayles of Lynn, Massachusetts, watched in absolute horror on that day in 1990 when the truck wheel crushed Yowser's front legs.

"I grabbed him, and his legs were battered and broken—just

dangling and bleeding," Ayles told the press. "I nearly went berserk because I love that dog."

The truck driver, aghast at the agony that his wheels had wrought, yelled at Ayles to jump in the cab with Yowser so he could rush them to a veterinarian.

The vet wrapped and splinted the spaniel's legs, gave him a tranquilizer, and suggested that Ayles take his pet to Angell Memorial Hospital in Boston for further examination and treatment. Ayles took the doctor's advice; Yowser had to be brought back and forth so many times that Ayles eventually got a baby stroller to expedite Yowser's hospital treatments.

A local newspaper photographer snapped a picture of poor Yowser all wrapped in bandages and being pushed in a baby stroller by his loving master.

"That caught everyone's eye," Ayles said, "and mail started pouring in from all over the world. It was heartwarming to know that so many people were concerned about the well-being of a lowly but loving pooch."

Ayles was delighted when he could announce Yowser's complete recovery.

Tramp Refused to Die

On May 3, 1991, a five-year-old, fifty-pound mongrel named Tramp found himself the target of a fiendishly cruel human who chained him to the back of a pickup truck and dragged him for nearly a mile. But Tramp was a fighter who wanted to live, and he endured eight surgeries and over five hundred stitches in his painful struggle to survive.

Tramp's owner, Sally Wright of Indianapolis, Indiana, was at work that afternoon; her husband, Cameron, had to leave the house on an errand. Before he left, Cameron chained Tramp outside so he could romp with the neighborhood children.

When Sally returned home about 3:30 P.M., she found the dog chain and surmised that one of the kids might have taken Tramp to play with him. Minutes later, she opened the front door in answer to Tramp's familiar scratching and was startled to find him covered with blood.

At about the same time, a neighbor ran up to Sally to describe the sadistic young man who had chained Tramp to the back of a pickup truck and had driven away, dragging the dog behind him. Bits of hair, skin, and blood marked the trail—until Tramp finally managed to slip out of his collar and escape.

During the course of a medical examination, it was determined that Tramp had lost nearly all of his skin. He had sustained serious burns over half of his body. One of his eyes had been nearly gouged out, and the pads of his feet had been scraped raw.

Veterinarian Sandra Norman said that it was the worst case of road burns that she had ever treated. She also observed that she had developed a sense that told her when a mistreated or injured animal would simply give up and die. She could tell that Tramp was not that kind of a dog.

Animal lovers in Indianapolis rallied to the support of Tramp and his owner. As word of the senseless act of cruelty spread throughout the city, checks came into the Wright home until $16,000 had been donated. That was the amount required to pay for eight major operations, five hundred stitches, and three weeks in an intensive care unit.

"It was touch and go those first few weeks," Sally Wright told reporter Dan McDonald. "People were so kind."

And Tramp rewarded his many loving supporters by recovering from his hellish ordeal and returning to his home with Sally and Cameron Wright.

Kelly the Cat Survives 46 Days in an Icy Storeroom

True, at seventeen pounds, Kelly was a bit on the plump side—but a forced starvation diet, incurred after being accidentally locked in a storeroom for forty-six days, seems like an extreme reducing plan, even for this tubby tabby.

Kelly probably has to assume her share of the responsibility. After all, if the storage compartment of her owner's coffee table had not looked so inviting a place to take a nap, she wouldn't have ended up in solitary confinement—without bread and water.

On December 8, 1989, while Kelly slumbered inside the coffee table with dreams of sugared mice dancing inside her head, her owner, Rhea Mayfield of Brownwood, Texas, asked her daughter Miken to help her move the table from their apartment to the building's storage room to make space for the Christmas tree. When they returned to their apartment, they noticed that Kelly was missing, but it never occurred to them that she could have been inside the table. Excitement over the approaching holiday season was replaced by anxiety over Kelly's welfare.

At last, concluding that she must have wandered out of the apartment while they were lugging the table to the storage room, Rhea called the police and placed ads in local newspapers. Every day, she would allot some time to searching the neighborhood for her missing animal.

It was not until January 22, 1990, over six weeks later, that the manager of the apartment building happened to hear the weak cries of a cat while he was in the storage room. It took him a few moments to locate the source of the pathetic cries, but he opened the compartment of the coffee table to discover a very hungry, very weak cat. Kelly had just enough strength remaining to rub her head against Rhea Mayfield's cheek and purr.

Kelly now weighed in at less than five pounds. She had lost an astonishing twelve and one-half pounds, three-quarters of her previous body weight.

The veterinarian who later examined Kelly suggested that the temperatures in the storage room, sometimes dropping several degrees below freezing, might actually have helped to save the cat's life by slowing down her body functions.

"A dog would not last a week without water," Tony Buffington, assistant professor of veterinary medicine at Ohio State University, told journalist Wayne Grover. "I've heard of cats lasting more than thirty days without liquid, but never forty-six. Kelly is one super cat."

Snowball Lives After a Two-Foot Arrow Pierces His Head

Carol Gingras of Middleboro, Massachusetts, returned from a Florida vacation in the winter of 1990 to find her five-month-old kitten, Snowball, skewered through the head with a two-foot arrow. Although Carol and her husband had left their white Angora under someone's supervision, some fiend had decided to use the kitten for target practice.

Dr. David Johnson, a veterinary surgeon, could tell from the wounds that the arrow had been inside the pitiful cat's head for two or three days. Three hours of delicate surgery revealed that the two-foot-long, quarter-inch-thick shaft had pierced Snowball's nostrils, traveled through his sinus cavities and throat, and exited through the back of his neck.

Dr. Johnson commented that the arrow was one and a half times as long as the kitten's body—and thicker than his leg bones. "If it had struck a hair above or below where it did, it would have hit the brain or spinal cord, which probably would have killed him," the surgeon told reporter Shelby Loosch.

Reflecting that the appearance of Snowball was "like something out of a horror movie," the dedicated veterinarian offered to treat the kitten for free.

After a second operation and a month's stay in the animal hospital, Snowball made a miraculous recovery. And once word of the cruelty worked on the kitten—and Dr. Johnson's selfless offer—had spread throughout the area, animal lovers donated enough money to cover the nearly two thousand dollars in medical expenses accrued by the vicious act of an anonymous archer.

Tessa the Turtle—A Pet for Five Generations of Missourians

Tessa the turtle may hold the record for being the world's oldest pet. In 1921, Missouri farmer Joseph Masek found her on his farm outside of the small town of Reform and carved his initials on her shell. Since turtles have hard-shelled portable houses, the act of engraving *JM 1921* on Tessa's back didn't hurt her at all.

Ten years later, Rudolph Masek, Joseph's son, found Tessa, noticed his dad's initials, and added his own to the scratchings on the shell.

Five years later, in 1936, Rudolph's son Floyd and his cousin Dave made their acquaintance with the friendly tortoise and took their pocketknives out to etch their personal marks on Tessa's shell.

More than half a century passed without any member of the family spotting the unique family pet, but then in 1988 the resilient turtle, who had been given up for dead, was found by Floyd's son Don. Remarkably, Tessa had continued to live on the Masek farm for at least sixty-seven years.

Old Tessa seemed to drop out of sight for another three years before sixty-six-year-old Floyd Masek found her again in June of 1991. With a bit of ceremony, he carved the initials of Don's newborn son Brandt on Tessa's timeworn shell. She had now been the Masek family's peculiar pet for seventy years.

Floyd's wife Bernice told newsman Michael Forsyth, "We love Tessa more every time we find her. She carries the history of the family on her back."

The Healing Power of Pets

Many men and women who suffer from various diseases and illnesses have observed how aware their pets become of their infirmities and how these animals come to play a protective role in their lives. However, as we have noted throughout the pages of this book, remarkable psychic linkups occur that permit pets to become more careful observers of the diversity of the human condition.

Now we shall relate some instances wherein the strange powers that our pets possess were channeled into dramatic acts of healing and physical salvation.

In July 1991, 58-year-old Shirley Smith of Bellevue, Ohio, had just returned from a week's stay in the hospital where she was diagnosed as suffering from congestive heart failure and failing lungs. The family cocker spaniel, Honey Bran Muffin IV, had long since accepted Mrs. Smith's physical limitations of deafness and blindness, but now he seemed to become immediately cognizant of his mistress's new condition.

During the night, Shirley awoke, unable to breathe and gasping for air. She knew that she was choking to death.

Awakened by the terrible sounds of gasping and distress, Muffin seemed to assess the seriousness of the situation and conclude that his master, Dallas Smith, was at a loss as to how to help Shirley through the trauma. Wasting not a second of crucial time, Muffin ran upstairs where the Smiths' thirty-year-old daughter, Karen, a medically trained respiratory therapist, lay sleeping.

Resentful of the intrusion into her sleep, Karen tried to shoo away the cocker spaniel. Irritated by the dog's nudges, she felt that Muffin had picked the very worst time to be playful.

When at last the determined Muffin's actions kept Karen from falling back asleep, the young woman became alert to the dog's intentions, and she heard the unmistakable sounds of a person choking. And in this particular instance, that person just happened to be her mother.

Karen rushed to her mother's room and employed her expertise and an inhaler to get Shirley breathing normally again.

There was no doubt in the mind of any member of the Smith family that Muffin had sensed that there was something drastically wrong with Shirley and had saved her life by awakening Karen to the danger.

Recently, through the ministrations of Baby, her mixed-breed dog, 47-year-old Bonita Whitfield was alerted to a serious skin cancer. In retrospect, Bonita, who lives near London, England, realized that whenever she was clad only in shorts or undies, Baby would begin to whine and attempt to bite her on the thigh.

Puzzled, because Baby was exceedingly gentle and never tried to bite anyone, Bonita scolded her dog dozens of times before she paid attention to the fact that Baby was seeking only to bite a mole on her thigh. She had never really noticed that particular mole, because it was toward the back of her thigh and out of her sight—but Baby seemed obsessed with removing the mole from her flesh.

Intrigued at last, Bonita felt the mole and became aware of a small lump. Over the next several months, she noticed the lump growing.

When she had the mole removed at King's College Hospital in London, Bonita was informed that it was definitely a malignant melanoma, but that the surgeons had removed it before it could spread. By pestering her about the mole, Baby had saved Bonita's life.

Dr. Hywel Williams, a staff physician in the dermatology department at King's College Hospital, acknowledged that the mole would have appeared completely normal to a lay person's untrained eye. Fascinated by Baby's preternatural ability to detect a malignant melanoma, Dr. Williams told journalist Esmond Choueke that he was planning to initiate a study to investigate whether dogs might be able to "sniff out" skin cancer.

Perhaps, Dr. Williams theorized, melanomas might emit a particular odor that dogs are able to smell. "If we are successful," he stated, "there may be a place for dogs in a screening process for malignant melanomas."

Whether such a universal application for dogs in the war against cancer will ever come about, Bonita Whitfield affirms her gratitude for her melanoma-detecting dog by giving Baby a huge hug each day.

Friend, a three-year-old golden retriever, serves as a full-time nanny at the Storey home in Englewood, Colorado.

Linda Storey, who suffers from multiple sclerosis, is confined to a wheelchair and has the full use of only one arm, but Friend faithfully provides her with his own strong and willing legs.

The retriever watches over five-year-old Jennifer and Matthew, the new baby. He picks up their toys, gently nudges them away from any potentially dangerous situations, and is there to hand Linda the telephone if she should need to make an emergency call to her husband Ken.

A "Lick of Life" from Inky and Buddy

Ever since she was trained for medical duties in 1986, Inky, a jet-black, ten-pound Chihuahua-mixed breed, has made three healing rounds daily at the fifty-bed Hospice of St. John in Lakewood, Colorado. With an uncanny instinct that directs her to the beds of those terminally ill patients who need her most, Inky has accomplished some of the most impressive emotional healing that the nurses at the hospice have ever witnessed.

Pam Currier, a former director of the hospice, told reporter Glenn Troelstrup that in many instances Inky could be more effective than a human therapist.

"To the lonely patient, Inky is a friend," Ms. Currier said. "To the depressed patient, she's a clown; and to the anxious patient, she's a diversion. Patients who have been on the receiving end of care for many, many months also find in Inky someone to cherish."

Hospice personnel have long been saddened by the number of patients who die without loved ones by their side. For such men and women, the perky presence of Inky is a true blessing.

Nursing director Rose Griffith stated that Inky brought ". . . life and humor back to the terminally ill, whose existence has been dulled by pain, fear, and loneliness."

Staff members have noted how Inky has a remarkable ability to ascertain the needs of the patients. "For those who really need her," Peter Wellish said, "Inky will spend the entire night. If there are two who need her, Inky intuitively will divide her time between them."

Sister Helen Reynolds of the Sisters of Loretto is given credit for the acquisition and training of canine therapists who work with the dying. Sister Helen wanted to find dogs that would not hesitate to jump into people's laps and to spread love impartially. She found such an animal in Inky, who was awaiting her own death sentence in an animal shelter.

"We'll never know how many patients died easier, how many grieving families were consoled, how many nurses were strengthened to carry on—all because of a bundle of love named Inky," said hospice director Sue Gallanter.

Buddy is another mixed-breed mutt who was saved from death row in a dog pound to brighten the life of gravely ill patients. Robin Tenny, director of the cancer unit at Desert Samaritan Hospital in Mesa, Arizona, stated that Buddy works wonders as he visits

198 STRANGE POWERS OF PETS

patients wearing such colorful costumes as an Uncle Sam top hat and a stars-and-stripes neckerchief.

Rescued from death by Robin and her husband John, Buddy had to pass rigorous tests before becoming qualified to join the elite ranks of eight thousand registered therapy dogs in the United States. Paula Cingota, head of the San Diego chapter of Therapy Dogs International, certified Buddy as Arizona's first therapy dog in the fall of 1991.

Robin Tenny commented that those patients suffering from terminal cancer are always in great pain. "But they glow when Buddy comes around. It's so exciting to see the smiles on faces that haven't smiled in days."

In the mid-1970s, tests were conducted in Great Britain in which the mentally ill were given a pet to look after. After a brief period of time, many patients showed an impressive degree of recovery. Several were able to resume their place in the outside world and once again to lead stable lives.

Dr. Larry Dossey, former Chief of Staff of Medical City Dallas Hospital, has said that the bonding between humans and animals would seem "to have survival value for humans; and studies suggest, indeed, that it is good for our health."

Dr. Dossey cites one medical study that demonstrated that closeness with a pet was the most important factor in predicting a patient's clinical course following a heart attack. "More important than any of the classic coronary risk factors such as smoking, high blood pressure, high cholesterol levels in the blood, or diabetes mellitus."

According to Dr. Dossey: "A growing body of knowledge has accumulated in recent years showing that close connections with animals is valuable for human health."

In September of 1991, California psychologist Sherry Lebeck revealed that she was employing two potbellied porkers named Louie

Louie and Sooey-Heart to cheer patients in her visits to senior centers, hospitals, and schools.

Ms. Lebeck stated that her two "assistant therapists" were especially effective in lifting the spirits of Alzheimer's patients.

In numerous instances, the psychologist said, patients who would not communicate with human therapists and counselors readily responded to Louie Louie and Sooey-Heart. Sooey-Heart is a special favorite because he allows people to touch him, flopping over on his side when his belly is rubbed.

Ms. Lebeck observed that many of her patients came from rural backgrounds. "So when they see a pig, we see an immediate reaction. The patients' long-term memories kick in, and they'll start telling stories about the pigs they remember from their childhood."

Montana, the Walking Doggie Blood Bank

Sarah Jacobs, a veterinary technician, who works at the Shandon-Wood Animal Clinic in Columbia, South Carolina, is justifiably proud of Montana, her massive, 162–pound mastiff, who has given over eighty pints of blood in the past five years. Ms. Jacobs figures that her pet's gift of life has saved about ten dogs a year since then, making a total of fifty canines walking around with Montana's vital fluid inside of them.

The six-year-old mastiff is so relaxed when he donates blood that he sometimes falls asleep during the twenty-minute procedure.

"Because of Montana's great size we can easily get a pint at a time," Dr. Neal L. Atkinson, head veterinarian at the clinic, told journalist Philip Smith. "We're not able to do that with smaller dogs."

Montana's blood has been responsible for saving a dog with a ruptured spleen and a dog that had ingested rat poison and was suffering from internal bleeding.

While most dogs would go into a frenzy if someone stuck a needle in them, Montana just lies there patiently when his mistress withdraws blood. "You usually have to anesthetize dogs for such a procedure," Ms. Jacobs pointed out. "But Montana doesn't even flinch. And he's never growled or tried to bite anyone when we take blood from him."

Incredible Accounts of Human Children Raised by Animals

Most of us have become familiar with Rudyard Kipling's tale of the boy Mowgli, who was raised by wolves in the jungles of India. Kipling's *The Jungle Book* was made into a live action feature with the actor Sabu in 1942 and was later translated into an animated musical version by Walt Disney in 1967.

The vast majority of people have assessed the claims that human infants have been raised by animals—à la Mowgli and Tarzan— and concluded that such accounts are quite likely to be the stuff only of adventure tales and children's stories. It is therefore quite fascinating to learn that there are well-documented accounts of animals becoming surrogate parents to human children.

For example, in 1920, the Reverend J. A. L. Singh, an Anglican missionary, who supervised an orphanage at Midnapore, India, discovered what appeared to be two real-life "wolf-children" when natives from the village of Godamuri sought his help in ridding them of ghosts. More intrigued than alarmed by the superstitious villagers, Reverend Singh had journeyed to Godamuri and, with several companions, constructed a tiger-shooting platform near a white anthill where the "evil spirits" had been seen.

After some time, three full-grown wolves emerged from a hole at the base of the huge ant mound. They began to stretch and to limber themselves for a nocturnal foray for food. The adults were followed by two pups.

And then, close after the pups, came a ghost—a hideous-looking being with hands, feet, and torso like a human, but with a large, grotesque head that was more like a big ball with a human face. Close at its heels came another awful creature, exactly like the first, although smaller in size.

Reverend Singh was suddenly left alone on the tiger-shooting platform. And when he returned to the village, he found that no amount of persuasion could convince anyone to return to the anthill to capture the ghosts.

In six days, he returned with help recruited from nearby villages and set about digging at the base of the huge anthill. Within a very short time, Reverend Singh and his men had flushed out three adult wolves, one of which was a female that stayed to defend her pups. The diggers had no choice but to kill the wolf in order to continue their excavation of the mound.

In a corner of the wolf den, Reverend Singh and his workmen found the two wolf pups and the two ghosts. The four creatures crouched together for protection and bared their teeth menacingly at the intruders. There, at last, were the two evil jungle spirits revealed for what they truly were: two young girls who had been raised by wolves.

The clergyman took the two wolf-children back with him to the orphanage at Midnapore where he undertook the arduous task of rearing them as human children. His first act was to cut the huge, matted mass of hair from their heads and trim their unkempt locks.

Reverend Singh estimated their ages to be about nine and two. He christened the older one Kamala, the younger, Amala. Neither of them was able to utter a single human sound. They walked about on all fours and could not be forced to stand erect. They growled and bared their teeth at strangers and preferred the company of dogs to humans.

The wolf-girls ate and drank canine-fashion by lowering their faces into their bowls. If not attended at mealtimes, they would scamper out to the courtyard and eat with the dogs, fighting with them for the choicest bits of raw meat and bone.

From their wolf environment, Kamala and Amala had developed a keen sense of smell. They could detect the bones and stores of meat that their canine comrades had buried. The girls not only relished the caches of rotting flesh that the dogs had hidden, but they would chase off any vultures they might spot beaking a choice bit of carrion.

Kamala and Amala slept most of the day, then prowled around at night while the rest of the orphanage slept. Whenever the opportunity presented itself, they would escape for a nocturnal hunt for small game in the surrounding jungle.

It was only after several months that the girls learned to tolerate loincloths. Personal hygiene was a major problem from the very beginning of their stay at the orphanage, for toilet training is incomprehensible to jungle creatures who follow the instincts of the pack.

Little Amala died eleven months after her capture, and Kamala gave evidence of her first human emotion when she shed a few tears upon the death of her sister.

Kamala began to respond to Reverend Singh's patient ministrations, relinquishing some of her ferocious, wolflike ways. With daily massage and measured exercise, she was eventually able to stand erect and to walk in a conventional manner. At one point her vocabulary included thirty words. Her table etiquette advanced to the point where she could eat at the table with guests who might be visiting the orphanage. By 1927, she was helping Reverend Singh by watching the younger children, and she had begun to attend church services.

Sadly, as Kamala's development in and adjustment to human society proceeded, her health began steadily to fail. On September 26, 1929, at the age of seventeen, the last of the wolf-girls died of uremic poisoning.

Such cases of animals becoming surrogate parents are rare; indeed, numerous cases of alleged "wolf-children" have proved to be retarded children abandoned to fend for themselves, not raised by wolves or other wild mammals.

In October of 1990, however, welfare workers in Springs, South Africa, discovered a strange case wherein the family dog, Skaapie, had apparently been given almost full responsibility for the care of Danny, a 23-month-old boy. The child's mother admitted that she had left her son in the kennel to be raised by the dog because, as an alcoholic, she was too drunk to care for him herself.

Child welfare worker Les Lancaster stated that the frail boy, naked and weighing only fifteen pounds, about half the normal weight for his age, scampered about on all fours, barked, and whined. It was obvious to Lancaster that Danny had spent so much time with Skaapie that he had assumed the behavior patterns of a dog.

Bonnie Rossolimos, a child welfare supervisor, said that she had cried for three days after observing Danny. She noticed marks on the blond, blue-eyed boy's neck that appeared to have been made by a dog collar. She, too, heard him making doglike noises and saw him crouching to eat.

In her defense, Danny's mother, Linda Hendricksen, 32, said that she did provide the boy with a bowl of food each day. But since she was not in a fit state to care for her son, she admitted to allowing the family dog to assume maternal duties.

"If Skaapie was like a mother to him, I was happy, because I couldn't cope," she told newsman David Barritt.

Sadly, when the officials took Danny away from his life in the family dog kennel, they also separated him from the devoted, caring Skaapie. Devastated by the loss of her human puppy, she died two weeks after their separation.

One of the most astonishing cases of surrogate animal parentage was made public in China's Liaoning Province in September of 1991 when researchers at the China Medical Institute in Shenyang revealed that sixteen-year-old Wang Xian Feng had been raised for four years by pigs. From age two to six, Xian Feng, ignored by her father, a farmer who wanted a son, and her mother, who was bedridden, lived in a pigsty and adopted the animals' behavior and their lifestyle.

The bizarre situation was discovered by a botany teacher with a penchant for rare flowers who came upon a small herd of pigs foraging for food in the mountains near Xian Feng's home. The teacher was astonished when he perceived that one of the pigs was really a small girl, who had been squealing, grunting, and shoving her face into the grass just like the members of her four-legged family.

Alerted to this arrangement, researchers from the Anshan Psychology Research Institute of the China Medical Institute went to investigate the truth of the botanist's claims. According to their report, they had even witnessed the six-year-old Xian Feng suckling a sow. In addition, they were amazed to see the child on all fours, grunting, pushing other pigs out of the way, and shoving her face into a trough to eat. At night, she would curl up next to the pigs to share their body heat against the cold.

The girl was removed from her home with the pigs and taken to the Institute for study and observation. There, an expert in dealing with children with learning problems was assigned Xian Feng as an ongoing project.

Although at first the child could only grunt and squeal, the patient teacher eventually taught Xian Feng to speak and to behave like a human being. Now, at the age of sixteen, she is thought to be a "sweet, simple, lovable" girl by all who know her.

An Unsettling Link

As eager as Sherry and her daughter Melissa were for their first trip to Sea World, they never could have foreseen its bewildering termination. Since they both loved animals and longed to experience the wonders of the mammals of the sea, they had looked forward to their California visit for years.

The weather was perfect the day they finally arrived. Melissa, at that time about age ten, and Sherry walked around the exhibits and carefully planned which ones they wished to see first, as it is quite possible to spend days there in order to see everything. They decided to start out with the dolphin performance.

Absolutely thrilled with the theatrics of the sleek, almost childlike sea creatures with the permanent smile affixed to their faces, Sherry and Melissa left the bleacher area at the show's end and headed for the dolphin holding tanks. A considerable crowd was gathering to hear one of the trainers answer questions.

Sherry, who was lost in thought about how exquisite and intelligent the dolphins were, was gazing at one particular dolphin in front of her. Totally unaware that the trainer was talking to her until someone tapped her on the shoulder and pointed at him, Sherry realized that she must have been mesmerized by the dolphin before her because she had not heard a word that had been said. Perhaps sensing this, the person who tapped Sherry said, "He's talking to *you!*"

Smiling, Sherry nodded her head and went back to watching the dolphin, which continued to bob straight up and down in the tank. Soon there was another tap on her shoulder, and the whole process was repeated—only this time people were also pointing at the dolphin.

Assuming that the people around her were noticing her fascination with the dolphin, she continued to gaze at the object of her attention.

Finally, a third time, tap-tap-tap. Sherry turned around, this time very conscious of the trainer on the microphone raising his voice at her in a very perturbed tone. Looking directly at her he said, "You don't want the dolphin to get hurt now, do you?"

"Well, of course not," she said.

The trainer continued to explain that although it was rare, there were some people who tuned in to a dolphin's frequency; and he told of a time at a different Sea World location when a telepathic link such as Sherry seemed to exhibit resulted in the serious injury of a dolphin. In its attempt to get closer to its psychic interlocutor, the dolphin scraped its skin on the rough-pebbled ledge at the tank's perimeter. An infection eventually set in and the dolphin died.

The trainer mentioned the vast amount of research intended to establish a commonality between dolphin sonar frequency and human speech. After his impromptu lecture, he asked Sherry, "You wouldn't want to harm the dolphin, would you?"

Shaking her head no, Sherry moved away. Nevertheless, she felt another tap-tap-tap. Slightly annoyed, she turned to hear a security officer say, "I'm sorry, but I've been asked to escort you out of the dolphin area."

"What did I do?" Sherry demanded an explanation.

The security guard told her that no one wanted to take a chance on the beautiful dolphin getting injured. "Come with me," he said with finality, and led them out of the area.

Sherry and Melissa then went to see Shamu, the killer whale. Noting the time for the next show, Sherry consoled Melissa with the promise of seeing the whales perform. As they were looking at the immense whales in the tank, one of the giant creatures came to the very spot they were standing and stayed there.

Sherry, somewhat dazed with all that had just transpired, was so touched by the whale coming over, hovering there in front of her and Melissa, that she unconsciously put her hand on the transparent plexiglas wall.

Thinking again of how strange it was that one dolphin out of many just kept on bobbing straight up and down in front of her, Sherry reflected on what she might have been thinking and whether or not she had sent any unconscious messages to the dolphin.

She decided she had been only admiring the dolphin. At the same time, she wondered what a dolphin saw when it looked at humans. She remembered staring into the dolphin's deep eyes when she suddenly became aware of the whale's huge eye and how intelligent and loving it seemed to be.

Now conscious that the whale was making some sort of sound and rubbing against the plexiglas wall separating them, Sherry was startled out of her reverie by another tap-tap-tap on her shoulder.

"I'm very sorry, Miss, but I have been asked to escort you *out of the park entirely!*" a security officer announced.

Her eyes instantly filled with tears, and she could barely choke out, "What did I do?"

Desperately asserting her innocence and explaining how long she and her daughter had planned for this day at Sea World—to say nothing of the fact that they had barely gotten use of the expensive day-long tickets—Sherry once more declared, "I didn't do anything wrong!"

Shocked to find herself outside the park with the security officer finally releasing his grip on her arm, Sherry noticed with great concern that her daughter was clearly upset by the officer's explanation of "no offense intended," that he was only following orders from top officials, that they must protect the priceless sea mammals.

When Sherry asked to talk to whoever had issued the command to have her removed from Sea World, the security guard refused and reiterated that he was just doing his job.

Left confused and unsatisfied, and feeling more like an accused saboteur than a mother fulfilling a promise to her young daughter, Sherry had no choice but to cut short their long-anticipated visit to Sea World.

In 1985, Sherry served as assistant to the late Dr. J. Allen Hynek, who was considered the dean of UFO research. Among his many other accomplishments, he was chairman of the Department of Astronomy at Northwestern University, as well as advisor to the director of the film *Close Encounters of the Third Kind.*

There were quite a few people who came through Dr. Hynek's center in Phoenix, Arizona, who were researching or sharing their stories and experiences of a dolphin-UFO link. One such person was a man named Daniel Fritz, founder and president of the Biogenics Foundation.

Dr. Fritz had studied with a Russian doctor behind the Iron Curtain who was pioneering the birth of babies underwater with the aid of dolphins. Research showed that babies born of such mothers, who spent time daily swimming with dolphins in a tank or the sea, were far more advanced on all levels than other children, and were more peace-loving and sharing. Sherry's understanding of this research was that dolphins were greatly more advanced than humans, possibly of extraterrestrial origin. What is more, such researchers theorized that dolphins were attempting to guide and to balance Mother Earth in the divine way assigned to them.

Sherry told Dr. Fritz of her Sea World experience, and many discussions about related matters with various friends and associates followed.

Some time later, several researchers with their own centers asked Sherry to work full time with the dolphins in similar projects as the one described in the Soviet Union. Sympathetic to the cause and the potential results, but feeling a slightly different mission, Sherry reluctantly declined the wonderful offer. Nevertheless, their dialogues continued.

Saved by the Skin of a Dolphin?

Sherry told the researchers about an experience in 1968, just off the coast of South Padre Island in the Gulf of Mexico. She was on the island, about as far south as was possible to drive, for the weekend, leading a Lutheran Church spiritual retreat for forty or so teenagers. They had all traveled together some distance in a cavalcade of cars and vans, and when they arrived, after setting up all the tents into a cozy little camp, everyone was eager for some free time in which to relax.

Sherry made a beeline for the beach and eagerly swam out beyond the breaking waves as far as she dared, then turned over on her back to float and to enjoy the blue sky and warm sunshine.

Perhaps a little too relaxed, she wasn't aware that the current had carried her so far out to sea that she could barely see the shoreline.

When she realized how far out she was, she calmly started to swim back to shore, occasionally treading water to get her bearings.

As she was treading water, suddenly she was jolted by something huge and alive knocking against her legs with such force that she was thrown off balance. Having been a lifeguard, she knew better than to panic, but it was all she could do to stay above water. Whatever it was kept on whapping her, and she went under several times.

Someone heard her screams for help and was about fifteen feet away from her when Sherry saw the look of panic on his face—as if he too had just been hit by the creature. He headed back for shore.

Sherry had gone under for at least the third time when, dramatically, someone else grabbed her and pulled her safely back to shore.

As her rescuer carried her out of the water, they both saw she was covered with blood. She was brought immediately to the first-aid ranger station, where she interrupted a line of people awaiting treatment.

Looking back, Sherry thinks she probably was unconscious, but she did register at least some of the ranger's words: he told her that he had removed a shark's tooth from her foot!

Asked if she wanted to keep the tooth as a souvenir, Sherry answered no, and passed out again. She was taken to the nearest hospital for shots and further examination, then released and told how fortunate she was. Fortunate nothing, Sherry thought—this was a miracle!

Arriving back at camp, Sherry appeared as though she had just returned from a major battle. She had been scraped from head to toe by the sandpaper-like skin of the shark, and, of course, she had a bandaged foot. Sherry was greeted by a thankful but somewhat disappointed group. While everyone was elated that Sherry was safe, they were unhappy with the ranger's announcement that the beach was off limits for at least several days, until it was deemed safe. This was the first shark attack that close to shore.

It took more than six months before Sherry could wear a shoe on the foot where the shark tooth was pulled out. But she's not complaining, Sherry says. If she had thought even for an instant that the creature was a shark, she knows she would have drowned!

Daniel Fritz was among the first to state emphatically to Sherry that it was most likely dolphins that had saved her from the shark—or sharks, more likely, as they travel in pairs.

Dolphins are the only living creatures in the water known to take on sharks and win. In fact, when a dolphin gives birth, a group from her herd surrounds the mother for shark protection. Other dolphins play midwife to the birth. After the mother has given birth, the circle remains in shark-patrol formation to baby-sit the newborn calf while the mother swims out of the circle for food.

Part Five

BECOMING ONE WITH YOUR PET

Real-Life "Dr. Doolittles" Who Talk to Animals

In 1984, Lou Bisconti, senior African elephant trainer at the San Diego Wild Animal Park, was being given a very pronounced cold shoulder by Sabu, the lead female elephant in the park. Not only did she suddenly choose to ignore his commands, but Sabu would turn her back and walk away from him whenever he entered the elephant yard.

According to *The Reader*, a San Diego weekly newspaper, Bisconti's wife urged him to contact a North County psychic-sensitive named Samantha Jean Khury, who communicates telepathically with pets and offers counsel to both animals and their owners. After five weekly sessions with Sabu and the other African elephants at the park, Ms. Khury brought about harmony between the trainer and his mammoth malcontents.

According to the psychic, Sabu and her fellows had a rather long list of grievances for Bisconti:

They were upset that deceased elephants were removed from the park before the others could observe their proper mourning ritual.

They were angered by the park's practice of separating baby elephants from their mothers.

They wanted more oranges and tomatoes and foods rich in vitamin C.

As the matriarch of the herd, Sabu had become increasingly anxious over the problems of the other elephants, and she expressed great relief when she was able to voice her complaints to Ms. Khury.

Ms. Khury informed Bisconti that she had done her best to explain to Sabu and the others that the personnel at the park were not deliberately trying to be cruel to the elephants and were conscientious in their attempts to care for them.

The trainer did his best to comply with Sabu's demands, and he saw to it that the requested oranges and tomatoes were brought in to increase the amount of vitamin C in the pachyderms' diet. To Bisconti's relief, his relationship with Sabu was restored to one of harmony after the giant matriarch held her conference with Samantha Jean Khury.

In her public lectures, Ms. Khury encourages all pet owners to communicate with their pets through "mental imagery." The key, she says, is to concentrate on the animal and think about its daily actions and habits. If the pet practices a habit that you would like to correct, visualize it acting the way you want it to do. Soon, she promises, the pet will begin to pick up the mental picture of your desire—and it will obey.

The slender, blonde psychic from Manhattan Beach, California, recommends that pets be assigned a job around the house or apartment to give their lives purpose and meaning. With a defined purpose, she states, a pet is less liable to tip over the garbage can, chew on your shoes, or sharpen its claws on the furniture.

Perhaps the most famous of the real-life Dr. Doolittles was a man named Fred Kimball, who definitely seemed to talk to the animals and to be able to understand them when they talked back. Meeting Kimball in Los Angeles some years back was a unique experience, and we remember him as a gentle, white-haired man who presented a strong image of frank sincerity.

Kimball said that pets are able to store up vast memory banks and that it was this information that he tapped. He claimed that it is not difficult to speak with dogs, because they use basic terms. When he communicated with canines, Kimball said that he used symbols to learn their problems and complaints.

"Dogs often complain because their masters do not demand enough of them," he stated. "Dogs like to be trained and active. Some even become a bit bored with their human family."

Kimball cautioned dog owners that when a dog appears merely to be sleeping in front of a warm fireplace, he may really have both ears tuned to family relationships. And what is more, dogs can remember things that happened in their human family in the past.

"I don't really *talk* to them," Kimball explained, referring to his oft-demonstrated ability to calm and apparently communicate with troubled domestic and wild animals. "I focus on their minds with mental telepathy. The animal has in its memory certain things that the owner may have forgotten. The animal gives me a mental picture of what it wants to say and then I 'translate' it for people. The language of animals is very much like the language of children."

A former wrestler, Marine jujitsu instructor, sharpshooter, champion swimmer, and merchant seaman, Kimball recalled his days many years ago with the Army Engineers in Panama, chopping roads through the heavy jungle.

"I seemed to have a 'jungle instinct,' as they called it," he told the Idyllwild, California, *Town Crier* for October 16, 1963. "I could sense when poisonous snakes were too close, so they made me lead man. That meant I was out in front with the snakes.

"We had snakes that hung in foliage at about the level of a man's head," he went on. "One strike from them and you didn't have long to live. . . . Because I could sense the snakes before we could see them, the men felt safer with me up front."

In the *Gardena Valley News* for September 29, 1963, Kimball admitted that it still seemed a bit strange to him to be able to read the mind of, for example, a sea gull. "Of course, most of the time they don't think too much," he admitted.

Kimball told of how he once "talked" a gopher out of its hole by offering it a yellow flower. First he tried to bargain for its presence by offering it some blades of grass—but the gopher held out for the yellow flower that stood just too far away from its hole to snatch in perfect safety.

A group of onlookers were amazed when the gopher came out of its hole and ate the flower from Kimball's hand. The creature retreated only when a four-year-old boy came too close.

"He said that he didn't trust the boy," Kimball explained. "He said the boy was too young to be responsible for his actions."

The real-life Dr. Doolittle stated that anyone can develop his or her senses and intuition to a higher degree to learn to communicate with animals. "The simple man finds his way out of the woods while the scholar gets lost," Kimball said. "The intellectual needs to listen more to his heart."

Kimball illustrated an extremely pragmatic by-product of being able to "talk" to the animals.

Once a friend in Florida needed some money in order to get married. Kimball talked to the horses at the Hialeah race track and picked fourteen winners out of the seventeen races.

"You can't always win them all," he said, shrugging off the three losses. "The horse may be on the level, but it may not have a good rider."

In Kimball's world view, modern men and women simply do not ask enough of Mother Nature. "The divine nature knocks gently at the door of your consciousness and does not force itself upon you. If one is not receptive or refuses to open the door, this divine nature recedes. Many people shut out a great deal from their lives because of their conventional fears."

Although Carole Wilbourn does not claim to be able to talk to her feline clientele, she has earned the appellation of the "Kitty Freud" because of her remarkable ability to help cats work out their emotional problems. Ms. Wilbourn, author of *Cats on the Couch*, says that she has successfully counseled ten thousand cats over a twenty-year period.

The Manhattan therapist states that she simply uses her background in human psychology and applies it to the behavior of cats. In her opinion, cats and humans are really not all that different. "They feel happy, sad, anxious, and frustrated just like humans," she told reporter Susan Fenton.

Although she had fully intended to apply her degree in psychology to assist human beings to survive the tensions of modern living, she found that she was being asked more and more often by friends to help them solve their cats' problems.

Susan Richardson of New York's Humane Society has declared Carole Wilbourn to be "a big help" with many of the cat behavior problems the Society has encountered.

Ms. Wilbourn once counseled a couple whose expensive paintings had suddenly become the targets of their cat's midnight marauding. She pointed out that their kitty was starved for the attention they were denying her by working late or partying.

The "Kitty Freud" advised their playing some prescribed cat games with their pet before its bedtime. The cat responded to their attention, became more contented and relaxed, and ceased attacking their works of art after lights out.

Incredible Encounters with Creatures of the Wild

Eighteen-year-old Lotty Stevens's incredible adventure began on January 15, 1990, when he left Port Vila, Vanuatu, in the South Pacific to go fishing. A raging storm set in, capsized his boat, and drowned the older man who had been his companion.

For three days, Lotty clung to the overturned boat; then, with only a lifejacket for support, he tried for two days to swim to land.

The teenager continued to pray for a miracle, fighting against fear and despair. Then he received an astonishing answer to his prayers.

With his eyes still closed, Lotty felt something big lift him from the water. There beneath him was a giant stingray, at least eleven feet long—with a six-foot poisonous tail—taking him on a "marvelous magic carpet ride."

At first Lotty was frightened, he admitted to journalist Chris

Pritchard. "But I soon began to think of the stingray as my friend. I patted it like a dog. Its skin was slimy, but its body felt hard and strong."

After several days of carrying Lotty, the creature suddenly dove and disappeared. Frightened and feeling very much abandoned, Lotty was terrified when his eyes scanned the sea and he spotted an enormous shark coming straight for him. Then he saw a second shark—and a third.

So that was why the stingray had dumped him. Although the marine creature was swift and powerful, it had probably got a good look at the vicious school of sharks in the vicinity and decided to make a run for safety. It had no doubt reasoned that it could not make a very quick escape with its human burden.

Lotty was stunned, then burst into tears of relief when his "angel" suddenly reappeared, swimming in a fast circle around him. Lotty had been wrong in thinking the stingray was afraid of the sharks. In fact, the situation appeared to be very much the opposite. The sharks turned and swam away.

Once again, Lotty Stevens was saved by the stingray, and he climbed back aboard its strong body.

The teenager survived by catching fish from atop his friend until the wonderful morning when he sighted land. The stingray headed for the shallow water and tipped Stevens off near the beach.

Lotty remembers staggering like a drunken man, then collapsing on the sandy beach.

The next morning he was awakened by a fisherman, and Lotty realized with great sadness that he didn't get a proper chance to thank his friend from the ocean.

A hospital on the main island pronounced him in good shape except for dehydration and sores.

His family was overcome with joy, for they had already held a funeral service for him. Over and over, Lotty Stevens said, he gives thanks to God for the wonderful stingray that saved his life.

In the remarkable story of Lotty Stevens and the stingray, we have a most unusual case wherein a totally undomesticated creature of the sea became an instant pet, companion, and savior. There are other

accounts such as that of the one detailed above that give moving
testimony to the Oneness of all life.

On June 2, 1974, Mrs. Candelaria Villanueva, 52, was on board
the *Aloha* when it caught fire and sank six hundred miles south of
Manila, Philippines. Unable to make it to a lifeboat, the woman was
tossed to the mercy of the ocean with nothing to keep her afloat but a
lifejacket.

Forty-eight hours later, Mrs. Villanueva was spotted by the
Kalantia, a Philippine navy vessel. The sailors who made the initial
sighting reported that the woman was clinging to an oil drum.

As the vessel drew near to the survivor and someone threw her a
life preserver, the men involved in the rescue noted that the oil drum
suddenly sank from view. It was only when the team was hauling the
woman up to the deck of the *Kalantia* that they saw she was clinging
to a giant turtle.

According to several international wire services, one of the res-
cuers remarked that "the giant turtle was beneath [Mrs. Villanueva],
propping her up. It even circled the area twice before disappearing
into the depths of the sea, as if to reassure itself that its former rider
was in good hands."

Mrs. Villanueva told reporters that after the *Aloha* sank, she had
floated in the water for more than twelve hours when a giant sea turtle
"with a head as big as that of a dog" appeared beneath her and lifted
her out of the sea.

Later, a very small turtle climbed upon Mrs. Villanueva's back as
she rode upon the giant turtle's shell.

"The small turtle bit me gently every time I felt drowsy," she said.
"Maybe it wanted to prevent me from submerging my head and
drowning."

On a late spring afternoon in 1990, brothers Daryl and Gary
DeGraffenreid found themselves struggling to stay alive in the turbulent, shark-infested waters of Channel Islands National Park off the

Southern California coast. Their small fishing boat had sunk, and Daryl, 30, and Gary, 32, had only water-ski vests to keep them afloat.

Daryl decided to swim for an island several miles away in an effort to bring help. As he desperately churned his arms and kicked his legs, he attracted the attention of a baby sea lion that came so close to him that the two of them made direct eye contact.

Suddenly Daryl found himself shouting at the sea lion, "Go get help!"

He may have momentarily felt ridiculous for telling his troubles to a baby sea lion; but Daryl wondered if he were just imagining that the creature turned and swam quickly away, as if it understood that the human struggling in the water needed assistance.

Daryl lifted his head above the waterline for a moment and saw that he really needed help—big time! Sharks had begun to circle him. And one of them was monstrous—more than twenty feet long.

"I was getting weaker by the second," he said later. "The swells kept coming, and I was going under each time. I was beginning to lose consciousness. The sharks were circling closer and closer."

Then, miraculously, fifteen to twenty sea lions suddenly appeared to form a wall of protection around him. "They were like a living barrier between me and the sharks!"

In spite of the bravery of the sea lions, Daryl found himself steadily sinking beneath the waves as his ski vest became waterlogged.

But as Daryl later told reporter Marie Terry, "God must have something very special in mind for us," for a Coast Guard boat with his brother Gary on board arrived to pull him out of the sea soon after the courageous sea lions had driven back the sharks.

Park ranger Don Morris said that it is common to have curious sea lions swim up to humans in the water, but he had never before heard of an instance where the sea-dwelling mammals had banded together to help one of their landlocked cousins.

In their book *The Strange World of Animals and Pets*, Vincent and Margaret Gaddis repeat a story first told by naturalist Alan Devoe concerning the experience of a man named Phil Traband who found himself pursued by a dangerous lynx while hiking through a woods.

Although Traband was understandably frightened, he stood still as the big cat approached him. Then, as he looked into the eyes of the lynx, Traband was struck by the "unmistakable look of a kindred spirit appealing for help." He could further see that the cat's mouth and muzzle were swollen and obviously causing it great pain.

Driven by some unfathomable inner-knowing, Traband stretched out a hand, and the big cat opened its mouth to permit a closer examination of its discomfort. Somehow, one of the lynx's fangs had pierced its tongue, which could not be released, thus causing a painful infection.

Traband remained in the energy flow of the Oneness of all life as he carefully worked the lynx's swollen tongue free of the fang that had impaled it. The big cat, considered dangerous, treacherous, and mean by experienced hunters, stood quite still in spite of what must have been excruciating agony.

When at last the infected tongue was freed, Traband gave the tawny cat an affectionate pat. It seemed to him as if a "glow of thankfulness" appeared in the lynx's eyes, and the big cat emitted a soft "mrroww" just before it disappeared into the woods.

The Gaddises conclude the story by asking rhetorically: "If man could remove hate and fear from his heart, then might this fundamental bond of affinity and affection bring beneficent cooperation between all the kingdoms of life?"

A Cry for Help from a Wild Bird

During the winter of 1973, Lorene Evans lived in a small rented house on Wabash Avenue in Fort Worth, Texas. One day as she was vacuuming the front living room, she heard a persistent sound above the mechanical humming noise of the vacuum cleaner.

"I finally turned off the machine and listened intently," she writes in the October 1991 issue of *Fate* magazine. "I heard nothing audible, but in my head I distinctly heard the crying of a small creature. I could feel its agitation as though it were desperate and calling for help."

Now that she had turned her full attention to the cry for help, Lorene felt that it was emanating from somewhere outside the house.

She put on her coat against the cold winter air and followed her inner guidance. She was "pulled" to the back of the house, then to the backyard near a corner of the house. Then she just stood there quietly, waiting.

"Just five feet away, I heard a flutter in the drainpipe," Lorene said.

During the summer, the pipe had been torn loose from the roof gutter, and now its spout was wedged tightly against the ground. Lorene pulled up the pipe and immediately discovered the source of the desperate cry for help.

There sat an exhausted little sparrow, "its eyes glazed over and its beak full of brown grass, the result of vainly trying to peck its way out after having fallen into the top of the pipe," she continued her account.

The bird seemed relieved, rather than frightened, by Lorene's appearance. He allowed her to pick him up and nestle him in the warmth of her coat pocket.

Lorene took the sparrow into the house with her and gave him some special solution by dropper. Next she made him a nest of a brown paper bag with a heating pad underneath.

The next morning, Lorene awakened to the sounds of chirps and pecks issuing from the paper bag.

When she came to inspect her overnight guest, she found that his feathers were all "plumped out," and he had a new sparkle to his eye.

She took the paper bag to the porch and set it on its side. "A healthy little sparrow hopped out, turned around, looked me right in the eye, and cocked its head as if to say, 'Thank you.' Then he flew away."

In a beautiful illustration of the Oneness of all life, that little sparrow had sent out a cry for help as it faced what would have been certain death. And Lorene Evans received the call and was able to help.

The Shamanic Sense of Kinship with All Animal Life

On some level of consciousness, all of us who love pets and wildlife have always known that there was a time in our ancient past when humans and animals enjoyed a much clearer communications link. In that less sophisticated era, devoid of science and our technology, we humans had to rely on our keen senses and our intuitive powers to stay alive. Furthermore, we knew that if we were to avoid becoming prey to the more powerful predators, we needed to become fast allies with certain of our animal cousins in order to survive the onslaughts of a deadly and hostile environment.

Utilizing innate mystical abilities, early humans developed a kinship with a particular animal life form that became to them what is known as a *totem*. The manifestation of the totemic animal served at times to warn of potential danger on the trail. On other occasions, the totemic entity warned of approaching illness or the death of a clan member. The totem could appear before others in externalized reality or it might only manifest in an individual's dreams or visions.

While there is much discussion among anthropologists and ethnologists over whether the totem animal could somehow attain such supernatural power or whether it served merely as a mediating vehicle for telepathically received information, most scholars agree that the Medicine Priests, the shamans of various tribes throughout the world, believed in a group mind, a kind of collective consciousness, that united them with the animal kingdom. Shamans believed in this common mind and felt it was possible to become an animal and to travel in a transmogrified form to accomplish magical deeds.

While even the more sensitive members of modern society tend to patronize animals and to place limits on their mental abilities, early humans universally saw themselves as brothers and sisters to the animal life around them. In those days of tribal existence, men and women participated in a very personal relationship with animals. Animals were by no means relegated to positions of lowly status. Indeed, most creatures were seen as possessing powers beyond humans and as existing closer to the essence of the Great Mystery.

As humankind began more and more to abandon a natural existence, it exchanged our communion with Nature and sense of Oneness with all lifeforms for alliances with our own kind that would eventually bring about mutual protection and companionship. What a tragedy it is that the great majority of humankind considered it necessary to widen the chasm between the artificial world of civilization and the natural world of animals.

As we now evaluate our prehistoric determination to separate ourselves from the natural order so that we might set about creating a planet of our own design, we see all too many negative by-products of that decision that appear to be poisoning us—as well as the Earth Mother and all of her animal and plant children. We pray that it is not too late—at least on the levels of mind and spirit—to re-enter the ancient realms that we once inhabited in primeval innocence.

"Animals live in realms of their own, realms totally different and far older than ours," wrote Vincent and Margaret Gaddis in their book *The Strange World of Animals and Pets.* "They possess senses and extensions of senses that we have lost or never attained. They see sights we shall never see. They hear sounds we shall never hear. They respond to terrestrial and cosmic rhythms and cycles that we have never charted."

Contemporary shamans and Medicine Priests believe that even today they can develop the ability to share the nonphysical world of animals and to blend with their consciousness. And each time they enter that ancient realm, they maintain, they can return in spirit to mythical times when the great separation had not yet occurred between humankind and animals. Each dance, each chanted prayer, each ritual, each deep meditation can return one to The Beginning, when humans and animals shared many paths to higher awarenesses.

A Vision Quest To Discover Your Totem Animal

The recognition of the Oneness of all life and the firm bond that exists between you and the four-leggeds, the winged ones, the creatures who move on their bellies, and the beings that live in the waters are vital elements in creating the proper philosophical frame of mind that will enable you to establish a firm psychic linkup with your pet.

In the Native American tradition, the totem animal served as a symbol of a special kind of spiritual relationship with a loving and caring guide. In the exercise that follows, you may be able to envision a manifestation of your personal totem animal, and with practice you will learn to employ that symbol to achieve increased awareness and a greater harmony with the Oneness of All That Is. In addition, you may begin to receive animal symbols in your dreams.

In order to assist you with an interpretation of your dream or vision, here is a brief list of the more common animal totem symbols and their general meaning in the cosmology of the traditional Indian Medicine Priests:

Bear: A sign of powerful mystical abilities as well as great physical strength, the bear also represents the solidarity of family and the steadfastness of loyalty to friends.

Bee: If this symbol appears to you as a totem or in a dream, recognize it as an industrious, selfless, self-sufficient energy that can achieve success in a wide range of activities.

Bird: A small bird appearing in your dream or vision most often indicates that a message of some importance is about to be delivered to you. Such a symbol can also represent your own ability to travel out of your physical body.

Buffalo: To receive an image of this great animal in your dream or vision is to receive a symbol of the force and strength that emanates from this powerful guardian of the Earth Mother. To perceive the buffalo as your totem is to experience a link with the elder spirits of the planet and to achieve a balance between the truths of yesterday and tomorrow.

Butterfly: The butterfly is a symbol of the inherent beauty in the transformational processes of life. The death of the humble, earthbound, crawling caterpillar brings into being the soaring expression of energy that soars on beautiful butterfly wings to the very heart of the Great Mystery.

Cat: There is a great duality inherent in this symbol. There is calmness and patience, but there is also a seething undercurrent of suspicion, perhaps even anger. The cat moves with grace, but also with caution. The cat can sit patiently awaiting its prey—but it can also leap into action in a split second.

Dog: The dog is a reassuring symbol of loyalty, faithfulness, and devotion to persons and principles. To possess such a totem or dream symbol is to know that there is a power outside of your own being that is ever ready to serve you and to come to your aid.

Eagle: The eagle presents a majestic symbol of the Sky Father, as well as an example of the life of isolation that must be the path followed by those who would seek the way of highest spiritual truths. The eagle people are those with a firm mission to serve only the loftiest of ideals. Be advised, however, that it can get very lonely on those mountain peaks.

Fish: A brightly colored fish may serve as a symbol that cautions you not to be distracted by the fanciful frills of life. Since fish live in the water, the universal symbol of creativity and the unconscious mind, pay careful attention to their actions should they appear in your dreams or visions. Their movements will assist you in assessing your creative powers.

Hawk: A symbol of benevolence from above, the hawk moves swiftly to accomplish its deeds. Those who have the hawk as their totem will find joy in being of service to others and in assisting their fellows to soar to higher levels of awareness.

Horse: Strength, health, a vigorous nature—all these attributes of the horse are cherished by those to whom this magnificent creature presents itself as their totem animal. The symbol of the horse encourages you to move ahead with confidence and to work steadily to create a positive future.

Lion, Mountain Lion, Cougar: The great cats represent courage, majesty, and respect, as well as strength and power on both the physical and spiritual levels. To have the mountain lion present itself to you as your totem is to be blessed with great mystical abilities.

Mouse: While the mouse represents a careful attention to detail, it also cautions you to look higher than your material possessions for true happiness. Very often, the appearance of a mouse in your dream is a sign urging you to expand your spiritual and mental awareness.

Rabbit: A symbol of virility and high energy, the image of a rabbit that appears as your totem animal or as a symbol in a dream indicates that you may be able to act quickly in order to avoid danger and to solve sudden challenges. However, you must always take an adequate amount of time to evaluate the true nature of the problem before you move "quick as a bunny."

Snake: Although the serpent universally provokes feelings of revulsion or fear, it is also a universal symbol for wisdom and the higher levels of spiritual development. Such a creature appearing in your dream or vision quite likely indicates that you are approaching a time of spiritual advancement.

Turtle: A sign of peace, patience, and fortitude, the turtle teaches you that great wisdom may come from moving slowly and deliberately. On the other hand, to act too slowly may gain you a reputation for being stubborn or moody.

Wolf: Independence of spirit combined with fierce loyalty toward family and friends is the essence of the wolf. Guardians of the night and the forest, these swift hunters take only what is necessary to their survival so as not to disturb the delicate balance of nature.

Here is a guided visualization that we have used at many of our seminars and Medicine Wheel gatherings throughout the United States and Canada. It has been extremely effective in assisting people to discover their special totem animal during a simulated vision quest experience, and it is one that you can use very easily.

The process is designed so that a trusted friend or family member can read it aloud to you. Or you may wish to prerecord the experience in your own voice so that you may serve as your own guide throughout the visualization.

We would recommend that in either case you select a recording of Native American flute and drum music to play softly in the background. If you do not have such a recording, then play some instrumental piece of music that you find moving or inspiring. Whatever music you do use, however, it should be devoid of lyrics, which might distract you from fully immersing yourself in the following experience.

Allow yourself to relax as completely as possible. When you have reached a very deep level of relaxation . . . when you have gone deep within the Silence Within . . . when you feel yourself moving toward the very center of your being, tell yourself that you have the ability to visualize in your mind the conditions of your vision quest.

(*When you have reached a point where you feel totally and completely relaxed, have your friend, family member, or your own prerecorded voice begin to read the following*):

Visualize yourself as a Native American man or woman on a vision quest. Focus your thoughts on the performance of some mundane, monotonous physical task.

Perhaps, like so many people on a vision quest, you have found a small clearing in the forest that has a number of rocks of various sizes at one end of the nearly barren area. In your mind, see yourself picking up one of the rocks and carrying it to the opposite side of the clearing. See yourself placing the rock down on the ground and turning around to get another rock.

See yourself picking up the new rock, carrying it slowly to the other side of the clearing—and then another rock . . . and another . . . and another. Back and forth . . . back and forth . . . over and over again.

Know and understand that you are performing this task for the sole purpose of depleting the physical self with monotonous exercise.

Know and understand that you are distracting the conscious mind with dull activity, that you are doing this to free the Essential Self within you, so that it can soar free of the physical body.

Feel your body becoming very, very tired.

Your body is feeling very heavy, very, very dull.

You have no aching muscles or sore tendons, but you are very, very tired. Your physical body is exhausted.

See yourself lying down on a blanket to rest.

Now, in a great rush of color and light, you are finding yourself elevated in spirit. You know that the power of love has taken you to a higher vibrational level. You have moved to a dimension where nonlinear, cyclical time flows around you.

From your previous limited perspective of Earth time, linear time, you are aware that you presently exist in a timeless realm in the Eternal Now.

Stretching before you is something that appears to be a gigantic tapestry, a tapestry that has been woven of multicolored lights, lights that are pulsating and throbbing with life.

The energy of the Great Mystery touches your inner knowing, and you are made aware that you are becoming One with the great pattern of all life.

In a marvelous, pulsating movement of beautiful lights and living energy, your soul feels a unity with all living things.

You see before you now an *animal*, any animal.
Become one with its essence.
Become one with this level of awareness within the Great Mystery.
Be that animal.
Be that level of energy expression.

Now see before you a *bird*, any bird.
Become one with its essence.
Become one with this level of awareness within the Great Mystery.
Be that bird.
Be that level of energy expression.

Now see before you a *creature of the waters*, any creature that dwells in lake, stream, or sea.

Become one with its essence.
Become one with that level of awareness within the Great Mystery.
Be that creature of the waters.
Be that level of energy expression.

See now before you a *serpent*, any creature that crawls on its belly.
Become one with its essence.
Become one with that level of awareness within the Great Mystery.
Be that creature that crawls on its belly.
Be that level of energy expression.

See before you now an *insect*, any insect crawling or flying.
Become one with its essence.
Become one with that level of awareness within the Great Mystery.
Be that insect.
Be that level of energy expression.

Know now that you are One with the unity of all animal essence within the Great Mystery. Know now that you forever bear responsibility to all animal life.

You are One with all things that walk on four legs, with all things that fly, with all things that crawl, with all things that sustain themselves in the waters.

And now one particular image is becoming very clear in your mind. The Great Mystery is showing you the image of one particular entity—an animal . . . a bird . . . a water creature . . . a serpent . . . an insect. Focus upon that single entity.

See its beauty. Become one with its beauty . . . its intelligence . . . its strength.

Blend with its spiritual essence . . . its power . . . its connection with the Great Mystery.

Know that this animal, this creature, is now your personal totem—that symbol which will often come to you in dreams and will represent the spirit of yourself on another level of reality.

Whenever you see this totem animal appear in your dreams, you will understand that it is a symbol sent by the Great Mystery to inform you that an important and significant teaching will soon present itself to you.

And now, at this moment in the energy of the Eternal Now, at this vibrational level of Oneness with all living things, at this frequency of awareness of unity with the cosmos, your spiritual guide will permit you to receive a great teaching vision concerning your relationship with all of life and your special and unique relationship with your pet. Receive this vision now!

(*Pause here for two minutes of silence in order to give the vision time to manifest.*)

You will now return to full consciousness at the count of five— filled with memories of your great vision concerning you and your pet. You will awaken filled with the image of your personal totem animal firmly set in your mind.

When you are once again fully conscious, you will feel morally elevated. You will feel intellectually illuminated. You will know that the spiritual essences of you and your pet exist beyond the physical plane.

You will no longer fear death. You will feel better and healthier than ever before in your life, and you will feel a great sense of unity with all living things.

One, returning to full awareness. Two, coming back to full consciousness. Three, filled with new knowledge, new awarenesses. Four, awakening filled with peace and love. Five, fully returned to complete consciousness!

Blending Psyches with Your Pet

We have previously noted that the scientific dogma of the Western world rejects any serious suggestion that animals may think and feel like human beings. And at the same time, it is alien to the Judeo-Christian religious tradition to grant an animal a soul. In at least this one question science and religion are united: It would be both unscientific and superstitious to believe that your pet has a soul.

While we intend no debate on the matter, we think it is of interest to note how Japanese scientists differ considerably from their Western counterparts in their attitudes toward animal research and primatology. According to an article in the March 2, 1991, issue of *New Scientist*, in Japanese culture there is no sharp, hierarchical distinction between God, humans, and animals.

"Animal memorial services, in which laboratory and field workers pray for the souls of animals that have been sacrificed to research, are increasingly common in Japanese research centers," states the article. According to anthropologist Pamela Asquith from the University of Calgary, Japanese scientists include material in their domestic publications that they remove from reports submitted to journals in the United States and Europe. These articles, according to Ms. Asquith, include what one Japanese scientist termed "living things"; that is, subjective descriptions of mental and personality traits of their animal research subjects.

Marita Royce, a metaphysical minister who resides in Sedona, Arizona, does not hesitate to express her belief that animals "absolutely do have souls," and she has even conducted formal funerals for pets.

"I gather the family around the grave," she explained. "Beside the body of the deceased, we lay a favorite blanket, toy, or some other object that had belonged to it. I acknowledge the Father-Mother God, and I express the family's gratitude for having been permitted to exchange love with the pet. I then encourage each member of the family to share some special aspect of the pet that was especially meaningful to that individual. I close the service with a recognition of the ascension of all life."

Ms. Royce believes that it is through our bond of love with our pets that we can help them to ascend to a higher spiritual level in the afterlife. "Through love, we can assist them to evolve."

Dr. Patricia Rochelle Diegel, an internationally known psychic sensitive, has stated that it is the love of humans for their pets that helps to bring the animals out of their group soul and sets them spiralling on an upward evolutionary trek. "The more an animal prefers human company," she said, "the more dissatisfied its soul energy will be to remain a cat or dog or whatever."

Dr. Diegel expressed her opinion that the current trend of giving one's pet a complete "set" of names—first, middle, and last—is a good one. "To bequeath your pet a middle name is to assist it to connect to the Higher Self and begin to move out of the animal kingdom. To share your last name with your pet, as if it were truly your child, a cherished member of your family, helps it to move to an even higher spiritual level."

We will permit our readers to come to their own resolution of the age-old question of whether or not their pets possess a soul. We certainly believe that there is some nonphysical aspect or essence that survives an animal's physical death, and we feel that it is that same spiritlike energy with which we can blend while we are sharing the Earth plane with our beloved pets.

Sheltering Your Pet Under the Umbrella of Love

If you will make a commitment to practice the following exercise on a regular basis, you will find an even stronger bond of love growing between you and your pet.

Sit quietly with your pet in a place where you will not be disturbed by external stimuli for at least thirty minutes. Calm yourself and attempt to clear your mind of all negative and troublesome thoughts.

Take a comfortably deep breath, hold it for the count of three, then exhale slowly.

Take another comfortably deep breath, hold it for the count of four, exhale slowly.

Take a third comfortably deep breath, hold it for the count of five, exhale very slowly.

Visualize a large umbrella that spreads itself over you and your pet. See the umbrella in a color that you associate with love. This umbrella of love will protect you and your pet from the bombardment of all rays of negativity. It will shelter you with love.

The moment that you have pictured you and your pet under the Umbrella of Love, stretch forth your hands over your pet and visualize the entire area around you being filled with golden light, thus creating around you and your pet your own mental and spiritual kingdom.

Visualize now a golden line of love that stretches from the top of your head and your pet's head and reaches up to the Great Mystery, God, the Source-of-All-That-Is. This is your lifeline of love, your loveline, and it provides you and your pet with a vital supply of loving energy. This loveline to the Great Mystery bonds you and your pet in a total and complete love relationship.

Visualize this loveline holding you erect when you are tired or feeling discouraged. You will instantly notice that your head goes up, your spine straightens. You will always remain strong and erect when you keep your loveline connected to the God Force.

If you should notice your pet appearing tired or distressed, find a quiet place where you can place your hands over its head and you can visualize its loveline reaching up to the Great Mystery and pulling its head erect.

A Great Teacher of Unconditional Love

Dale W. Olson of Eugene, Oregon, author of *Knowing Your Intuitive Mind*, was privileged to enjoy a complete and loving relationship with a German shepherd-Norwegian elkhound mix named Ananda and known as Nanda Dog.

"Nanda Dog was a total love bug," Olson said, "and we entered into an incredibly deep rapport. In addition, he was remarkably intelligent. In repeated experiments that I conducted, he could distinguish between various colored balls. He also barked at traffic lights whenever they turned from red to green if I might hesitate to go forward."

A large animal, Nanda Dog remained exceedingly gentle, and he could be trusted to herd stray chickens out of the flower garden and return them carefully to their coop.

At that time, Olson had a construction business, and Nanda Dog would come by the site where he was working and bravely climb sixteen-foot ladders to join his master on the roofs of the partially constructed homes. Nanda Dog could also turn doorknobs and unlock deadbolts.

"One time Nanda Dog showed up at a construction site where there were a number of chickens wandering in and out of the work area," Olson said. "I told Nanda Dog that he couldn't even *look* at those chickens. A little while later, I glanced down at him and saw him looking up at me with pleading eyes. A rooster had perched itself on Nanda Dog's butt, but he was obeying me and not even looking at it."

Olson knew that Nanda Dog strongly felt the call of the wilderness, that there were wolflike impulses deep within him.

"One time when we were driving in a thickly forested area during the night of the full moon, I suddenly had an impulse to stop the van and to get out with Nanda Dog," Olson told us. "All of a sudden, I found myself howling at the moon with Nanda Dog."

After a brief time, a beautiful silver wolf appeared at the edge of the forest. "I knew that the wolf had come to present Nanda Dog with the call of the wild. The two of them left together. I understood. It was as if I could feel that same urge within myself.

"But I feared for my friend," Olson continued. "Things were different in the wilderness. I hoped that he would not be attacked. I called for him for over an hour before he returned to me. I hugged him and talked to him. Then he jumped back into the van and fell into a deep sleep. As I drove into the night, I could hear him whimpering, making puppy noises as he re-enacted his adventure in his dreams."

236 STRANGE POWERS OF PETS

Once while they were whitewater rafting, the craft on which Olson and Nanda Dog rode capsized in turbulent water. "There was a heavy undertow, and I was pulled down. I thought that I would surely drown. In my flailing about I could see that Nanda Dog had made it to the shore. I was grateful that he would live."

But certainly the strong bond of love that existed between them could not have permitted Nanda Dog to watch his master drown. The big dog plunged back into the river, swam to Olson, and extended his tail to him.

"I understood his meaning," Olson said, "and I grabbed his tail and allowed Nanda Dog to pull me to shore."

Olson sat on the bank, telling Nanda Dog over and over that he had saved his life. "But he just kept licking my face!"

Sadly, as in all stories about devoted pets, there comes that awful time when the animal no longer returns to loving arms.

"I was living on Bear Mountain," Olson said. "I think Nanda Dog might have got between a mama bear and her cubs. I offered a thousand-dollar reward, and I waited months and months before I finally gave up hope of ever again seeing my friend in the physical."

Since that time, Olson has stated that he has felt Nanda Dog's etheric body snuggling up against him in bed at night, and he has felt his doggy kisses on his cheek. "Nanda Dog taught me more about unconditional love, caring, and compassion than all the books that I have ever read on the subject," Olson said, tears flowing with the memory of his beloved Nanda Dog. "I hope that someday I can find a canine friend as great as he was."

Becoming One with Nature

Here is an exercise that can help you to grow in greater balance with nature and to walk in greater harmony with the Earth Mother. You might try it the next time that you are walking with your pet in the woods, the beach, the desert, or in a city park. If you practice this exercise in your home or apartment, visualize yourself standing somewhere in nature.

Take a comfortably deep breath, hold it for the count of three, then release it. Repeat this three times.

Look toward the North. Let your eyes go to the far, far horizon of the North. Feel yourself growing as you look toward the North.

Visualize yourself stretching upward, as if you were a tall tree. Stretch your arms out in front of you as if they were tree limbs stretching forth.

Imagine that you can touch the far horizon of the North. Then, turning slowly, imagine that your arms stretch out and touch the horizon, the great pole of the horizon. Feel your fingertips touching the very farthest reaches of the horizon as you begin to move slowly around in a counterclockwise circle.

Perhaps your fingertips touch a forest . . . a cloud . . . an ocean wave . . . the shoreline of a lake . . . the rolling grasses of a plain. Wherever you touch, as you move slowly with your arms stretching from horizon to horizon, let the Earth Mother know that you are aware of her. Bless her and all that you touch. Ask the Earth Mother to bless you and your pet. Ask the Earth Mother to guide the two of you to walk together in harmony, peace, and love.

Keep your eyes open as you move counterclockwise. Feel your fingertips brush the farthest reaches that you can see with your eyes.

Now close your eyes and know that you and your pet are focal points for energies from a higher source. There is the Earth Mother all around you. There are the heavenly energies above you. And all around you are the seen and unseen energies of the Great Mystery.

You, through your mind, constitute the focal point that touches the Universe, that caresses the Earth Mother. Open all of your senses to receive the blessing that the Earth Mother sends back to you.

Feel yourself and the spirit essence of your pet blending together and becoming One with All That Is. Feel and know that the two of you have become the center of a great benevolent energy that is consecrated by all that surrounds you.

238 STRANGE POWERS OF PETS

Becoming One with Your Pet

Sit quietly with your pet in a place where you will be undisturbed for at least thirty minutes. Calm yourself and attempt to clear your mind of all negative and troublesome thoughts.

Take a comfortably deep breath, hold it for the count of three, then exhale slowly. Repeat this procedure three times.

Begin to focus on the thought that you and your pet are one in mind and spirit. Form a mental picture of the two of you in perfect harmony.

This mental picture must make no reference to any of your pet's negative habits. This ideal picture must not contain any image of any aspect of your pet's behavior that you might wish to modify or change. You must focus only on that ideal image of the two of you in perfect harmony and in a complete love relationship. You must believe with all your soul essence that you are now living in the perfect blending of Oneness.

Once you have fashioned the image of you and your pet melding perfectly into a Oneness of mind and spirit, hold that picture fast and begin to inhale very slowly, taking comfortably deep breaths.

As you inhale, you are drawing in what the mystics refer to as the *mana* or the *prana* and what martial artists refer to as the *ki* or *chi*, the all-pervasive life force. This is the energy of miracles, and it will permit you to shape the ideal condition of Oneness with your pet.

Create and hold fast in your mind the picture of your perfect Oneness with your pet as you inhale and draw in the *mana*. The *mana* will give the image enough strength to hold together while your soul begins to materialize the picture into physical actuality.

Hold the picture firmly in your mind as you continue to breathe slowly, sending vital energy to your soul.

Be *alive* in the picture.

Feel it.

Keep your mind from all negative thoughts and permit the perfect harmony of complete Oneness with your pet to continue to grow.

Once you work steadily at achieving a oneness with your pet, you will enter a beautiful realm of understanding in which you will see very clearly that the strange powers of pets manifest most profoundly in the energy of love that we two-leggeds have always the choice of sharing with our brothers and sisters among the four-leggeds, the winged ones, the beings that crawl on their bellies, and the creatures who live in the waters. Once we learn to express respect rather than condescension, and love rather than ownership, we too shall greatly expand our own powers of spirit.